THE
PLAGUE

OTHER TITLES IN THE GREENHAVEN PRESS LITERARY COMPANION SERIES:

THE GREENHAVEN PRESS
Literary Companion
TO WORLD LITERATURE

READINGS ON

THE PLAGUE

Jesse G. Cunningham, *Book Editor*

Bonnie Szumski, *Series Editor*

Greenhaven Press, Inc., San Diego, CA

Every effort has been made to trace the owners of copy-righted material. The articles in this volume may have been edited for content, length, and/or reading level. The titles have been changed to enhance the editorial purpose. Those interested in locating the original source will find the complete citation on the first page of each article.

Library of Congress Cataloging-in-Publication Data

Readings on The plague / Jesse G. Cunningham, book editor.
        p. cm. — (Greenhaven Press literary
companion to world literature)
    Includes bibliographical references and index.
    ISBN 0-7377-0691-0 (lib. bdg. : alk. paper). —
ISBN 0-7377-0690-2 (pbk. : alk. paper)
    1. Camus, Albert, 1913–1960. Peste. 2. Algeria—In
literature. 3. Plague in literature. I. Title: Plague.
II. Cunningham, Jesse G., 1969–   III. Greenhaven Press
literary companion to world authors.

PQ2605.A3734 P438 2001
843'.914—dc21   00-069508
                                                       CIP

Cover photo: Archive Photos, Hulton Getty Collection, Kurt Hutton Photographer (1952)
Library of Congress, 16

Copyright © 2001 by Greenhaven Press, Inc.
PO Box 289009
San Diego, CA 92198-9009
Printed in the U.S.A.

"What these fighters, whose experience I have to some extent translated, did do, they did in fact against men. . . . They will do it again, no doubt, when any terror confronts them, whatever face it may take on, for terror has several faces."

—Albert Camus

CONTENTS

FOREWORD

"'Tis the good reader that
makes the good book."

Ralph Waldo Emerson

The story's bare facts are simple: The captain, an old and scarred seafarer, walks with a peg leg made of whale ivory. He relentlessly drives his crew to hunt the world's oceans for the great white whale that crippled him. After a long search, the ship encounters the whale and a fierce battle ensues. Finally the captain drives his harpoon into the whale, but the harpoon line catches the captain about the neck and drags him to his death.

A simple story, a straightforward plot—yet, since the 1851 publication of Herman Melville's *Moby-Dick*, readers and critics have found many meanings in the struggle between Captain Ahab and the whale. To some, the novel is a cautionary tale that depicts how Ahab's obsession with revenge leads to his insanity and death. Others believe that the whale represents the unknowable secrets of the universe and that Ahab is a tragic hero who dares to challenge fate by attempting to discover this knowledge. Perhaps Melville intended Ahab as a criticism of Americans' tendency to become involved in well-intentioned but irrational causes. Or did Melville model Ahab after himself, letting his fictional character express his anger at what he perceived as a cruel and distant god?

Although literary critics disagree over the meaning of *Moby-Dick*, readers do not need to choose one particular interpretation in order to gain an understanding of Melville's novel. Instead, by examining various analyses, they can gain

9

numerous insights into the issues that lie under the surface of the basic plot. Studying the writings of literary critics can also aid readers in making their own assessments of *Moby-Dick* and other literary works and in developing analytical thinking skills.

The Greenhaven Literary Companion Series was created with these goals in mind. Designed for young adults, this unique anthology series provides an engaging and comprehensive introduction to literary analysis and criticism. The essays included in the Literary Companion Series are chosen for their accessibility to a young adult audience and are expertly edited in consideration of both the reading and comprehension levels of this audience. In addition, each essay is introduced by a concise summation that presents the contributing writer's main themes and insights. Every anthology in the Literary Companion Series contains a varied selection of critical essays that cover a wide time span and express diverse views. Wherever possible, primary sources are represented through excerpts from authors' notebooks, letters, and journals and through contemporary criticism.

Each title in the Literary Companion Series pays careful consideration to the historical context of the particular author or literary work. In-depth biographies and detailed chronologies reveal important aspects of authors' lives and emphasize the historical events and social milieu that influenced their writings. To facilitate further research, every anthology includes primary and secondary source bibliographies of articles and/or books selected for their suitability for young adults. These engaging features make the Greenhaven Literary Companion Series ideal for introducing students to literary analysis in the classroom or as a library resource for young adults researching the world's great authors and literature.

Exceptional in its focus on young adults, the Greenhaven Literary Companion Series strives to present literary criticism in a compelling and accessible format. Every title in the series is intended to spark readers' interest in leading American and world authors, to help them broaden their understanding of literature, and to encourage them to formulate their own analyses of the literary works that they read. It is the editors' hope that young adult readers will find these anthologies to be true companions in their study of literature.

INTRODUCTION

How does one meaningfully exist in a meaningless universe? A quest for answers to this metaphysical condition of humanity characterizes the literary work of Albert Camus. For Camus, the struggle to reconcile a meaning for life in an existential vacuum was the condition of the absurd. *The Plague* offers some positive responses to this seemingly hopeless struggle.

Originally published in 1947 in the post–World War II environment of France, *The Plague* is a multilevel work. Noted for its straightforward plot, this novel presents itself as a chronicle of one city's fight against a deadly disease. The narrator, an anonymous participant until he reveals his identity at the end of the chronicle, documents the outbreak of the disease, its horrible toll among the population, the city's response to the epidemic, and finally the plague's recession. Although the narrator's vivid accounts of the plague's ravages are enough to compel a contemporary reader more than a half century after the book's initial publication, Camus's novel extends beyond the surface level of the plot.

Camus intended *The Plague* as an allegory of the Nazi occupation that he experienced firsthand while living in Paris after the German conquest of France. To Camus, these invaders were the plague, and many of the novel's characters represent the underground French resistance freedom fighters who struggled against Nazi oppression (other characters are analogues for those who chose to collaborate with the enemy). In fact, Camus himself was a member of the resistance movement, and although he often downplayed his own role, there is no doubt that he risked his life fighting for a cause that was fatal for some of his colleagues. This allegorical level lends the novel a great historical significance worthy of attention, but Camus extends the meaning of *The Plague* beyond that specific context: The plague signifies not only the Nazis or any other totalitarian regime but also the general evil of oppression and the absurdity of the meaning-lessness of life. In this reading, the best possible response is to rebel against the oppression, the evil, and the absurdity. *The Plague*, therefore, is relevant to contemporary readers for these broader applications.

This literary companion to *The Plague* reflects the variety of critical views elicited by Camus. Some critics, including many of his contemporaries, question the effectiveness of the plague symbol and its function in the allegory; others defend the allegory by pointing out the novel's extended meanings. Also of academic interest are the technical aspects of narrative and structure. Many scholars contemplate the political, social, and philosophical themes of *The Plague*, insisting that in order to decipher meaning from the novel, it must be correlated with some of Camus's other works: *The Myth of Sisyphus*, a lyrical essay that provides a working definition for the absurd; *The Stranger*, which is a fictional illustration of an individual's struggle against absurdity; and *The Rebel*, an essay on revolt intended by Camus to complement *The Plague*. These scholars see an evolution from *The Stranger* and its concerns over the individual to a prescription for collective revolt against the absurd in *The Plague;* they suggest that the solidarity of social action in itself provides a meaning for life.

More than fifty years since its publication, *The Plague* remains an effective work on all of these levels. As an account of dehumanizing destruction, it has the capacity to strike fear in the heart of the reader; as an allegory, the novel informs a contemporary audience of a shocking and indelible historical event. Ultimately, *The Plague* inspires its readers with its implicit call to struggle against oppression in any form, whether it be the oppression of despotism or the ravages of a horrible disease such as the AIDS epidemic. In the end, one finds meaning in the collective effort to resist these manifestations of the absurd.

Albert Camus: A Biography

On November 7, 1913, Albert Camus was born in Mondovi, a small village in the French colony of Algeria. His father, Lucien, worked for the Ricôme wine company, living on its farm with his wife, Catherine, and their first son, also named Lucien. Catherine's family was Spanish in origin, and Lucien was descended from the original French colonists; the family was designated as *pied-noir*—European descendants born in Algeria—and Albert would always identify with these roots.

He grew up in a multicultural environment, Algiers being inhabited by Arabs, Berbers, and the more recent groups of European immigrants. Ethnic tensions flourished between the naturalized French population and the native Algerians, who resented the colonization of their land (since 1830) and the years of unjust sociopolitical oppression at the hands of the government.

The Early Years

When Albert was only eight months old, his father was re-activated into the soldiery, shipping out when Germany declared war on France in August 1914. Albert never saw his father again, Lucien falling as one of the first French casualties in the Battle of the Marne. Shortly before her husband's death, Catherine and her sons went to live in the cramped conditions of her mother's apartment in Belcourt, a working-class neighborhood in the city of Algiers. The family lived in poor conditions. Catherine supported herself and her children by working as a cleaning woman, her wages supplemented by a stipend awarded to war-widowed mothers. Catherine had a considerably more mild parenting approach than the stern Madame Sintès, who shared this responsibility with her daughter, often serving as the primary caregiver while Catherine and her brothers, Etienne and Joseph, worked long, rigorous hours to support the family.

Madame Sintès and Catherine, who was hearing- and speech-impaired, were illiterate, so they could not introduce the future writer to the world of words.

The Camus boys were entitled to governmental aid for education, so Albert started attending elementary school in 1918. He came under the wing of Louis Germain, who displayed a personal interest in Albert's budding academic career. Germain wanted to nurture his student's potential and encouraged him to attend high school, which would not be covered by the stipend. Germain convinced Catherine, who worried about the cost of tuition and was pressured by her mother to put ten-year-old Albert to work like his brother, that Albert would perform well enough on the entrance exams to earn a scholarship that would cover expenses, which the boy did after Germain devoted extra hours to coaching him.

In October 1924 Albert entered high school and began his general education. According to biographer Oliver Todd, the students were taught the French establishment's perspective of colonialism as a positive force, which portrayed "France as benefactor, civilizer, and enlightener of its colonies."[1] From an early age, Albert developed an interest in philosophy and knew that he wanted to become a writer, though his family expected him to become a schoolteacher. He participated in sports, excelling in soccer as a ferocious competitor. Encouraged by his grandmother, Albert eventually labored for an ironmonger and then a maritime broker during school vacations.

In August 1930 Camus began suffering frightening symptoms, running fevers, and often spitting blood after coughing fits wracked his body. As a war orphan, he was entitled to free medical treatment, and the doctors diagnosed the sixteen-year-old with tuberculosis, a disease with lethal implications at that time. With limited medical knowledge available, the doctors forcibly collapsed the teenager's infected right lung, hoping that the tubercular lesions would heal while the lung recovered. Albert would be ravaged by attacks of this disease for the rest of his life; his experiences with tuberculosis would later provide material for *The Plague*.

Recuperating, the stricken Camus went to live with his mother's sister, Antoinette, and her husband, Gustave Acault. Although most of Camus's family were illiterate, Gustave, a butcher, had intellectual interests, and he introduced

Camus to the works of writers such as Fyodor Dostoyevsky and André Gide. Gustave engaged Camus in ideological discussions, treating him as an adult and exposing him to new concepts. During his stay, Camus came to see Gustave as a father figure.

Concerned by Camus's prolonged absence, philosophy teacher Jean Grenier convinced the young man to resume his studies. With his tuberculosis in remission, Camus returned to school in October 1931, shortly before turning eighteen. He flourished under his new mentor's guidance, graduating in June 1932. Camus and Grenier began a lifelong friendship, and Camus would later credit Grenier for his intellectual and artistic formation.

YOUNG ADULTHOOD

Grenier exposed Camus to many works of literature and philosophy, including those of Marcel Proust, Leon Chestov, and Friedrich Nietzsche. The teacher held lengthy discussions with the young man about Grenier's own recent work, *Les Iles*, a long philosophical essay that dealt with themes such as heroism and revolt. Camus was impressed by the literary style in Grenier's essay. Camus began publishing locally, writing a number of essays for the literary magazine *Sud.*

Meanwhile, Camus had been courting Simone Hié during these years. The relationship proved to be troubled early on. For one thing, Uncle Gustave did not approve of his nephew's new girlfriend. More troublesome still, Camus discovered that Hié had been addicted to morphine since her early teens. Camus mistakenly thought that he could save Hié from a life of substance abuse; despite his attempts to progressively wean her from dependency, she remained an addict. Another complication in their relationship was that the attractive Hié provoked much attention from men, which made young Camus quite jealous. Despite these problems, Camus and Hié married on June 16, 1934, and the couple, supported financially by their relatives, moved into their own apartment.

Not long before his wedding, Camus had entered the University of Algiers. At the university Camus took classes in history and literature as well as courses in philosophy taught by René Poirier and Grenier. Among the hundreds of books he read at this time, the young Camus was deeply impressed by André Malraux's acclaimed *La Condition Humaine.* This writer replaced even Gide as Camus's chief literary hero. Malraux would remain Camus's idol among contemporary writers for the rest of his life.

It was also at the university that Camus was exposed to radical politics. Camus, already sensitive to the rights of workers, was encouraged by Grenier and other friends to join the Communist Party in 1935. Camus associated with a circle of Algerian intellectual liberals who were con-

Albert Camus

cerned about sociopolitical inequalities and bitterly opposed to the rise of anti-Semitism and Fascism in Europe. Camus's hero, Malraux, visited Algiers in July 1935 and spoke about these topics. Malraux was popular with Camus's fellow students, whom he encouraged in political activism.

Camus received his degree in May 1936 after writing a thesis comparing the mystic philosophers Saint Augustine and Plotinus. What he would do after receiving his degree remained open to question, however. Camus's history of bouts with tuberculosis thwarted his plans for teacher certification. Moreover, although military service was compulsory for young men, Camus was exempted due to his health.

The summer of 1936 not only marked the end of Camus's university days but also the end of his marriage to Simone. In early July Camus embarked on a vacation in Europe with Simone and a friend, Yves Bourgeois, but the trip proved to be a disaster. To begin with, illness forced Camus to travel separately from his wife and friend, who had planned to spend much of the vacation kayaking on rivers in Austria, Czechoslovakia, and Germany. Worse, however, Camus found a letter addressed to Simone that contained evidence that she was having an affair with a doctor who supplied her with drugs. Upon their return to Algiers in September, Simone and Albert immediately separated. Their divorce would not be finalized for another four years, but the marriage was effectively over. The unhappy experience quickly was incorporated into Camus's work, for he soon began to draft a novel, *The Happy Death*, in which the protagonist is betrayed by an unfaithful woman.

Camus escaped his unhappy personal life by immersing himself in theater and politics. He was a founding member of a troupe called the Théâtre du Travail, acting as director, producer, actor, and writer. Members of this troupe were motivated both by a love for literature and a desire to publicly express their emphatic leftist political views. For example, their first production was Camus's adaptation of Malraux's *Days of Wrath*, in which a German Communist is persecuted by the Nazis. The group managed to outrage some powerful opponents of the Communists. The next production, *Révolte dans les Asturies*, largely written by Camus, was banned from performance by the right-wing mayor of Algiers.

Despite his leftist views, Camus's relationship with the Communist Party was destined to end. While serving the party as the secretary-general of the Algiers Cultural Center, Camus became embroiled in political infighting over the issue of national liberation for Algeria. Camus and other leftists sought to equalize the social differences between the European colonists and the Arabs who constituted the majority in Algeria. Camus favored a policy that would grant Muslims the right to vote, but he found that his fellow Communists were largely opposed to the Algerian independence movement, which they denounced as overly nationalist. Camus was also at odds with other Communists over the fact that the Théâtre du Travail was producing some plays not approved by the Communist Party, so he founded a politically independent troupe called the Théâtre de L'Equipe. Refusing to resign his party membership, Camus was expelled shortly after July 1937; the falling-out ended for life the affiliation of Camus and the Communists.

While his flirtation with Communism was coming to an end, Camus continued to pursue his literary interests. His first book, *L'Envers et l'endroit*, containing five essay-novellas, was published in a limited edition of 350 copies. At the same time, Camus was at work on another novel, titled *The Stranger*. For this work he drew on parts of his still unpublished novel, *The Happy Death*.

Also during this time, Camus started his career in journalism by working for Pascal Pia, the managing editor of the *Alger Républicain* and its smaller companion paper, *Le Soir*

Républicain. Politically, Camus and his boss saw eye-to-eye. Both opposed anti-Semitism and fascism, and both wanted to see an end to the social inequalities between Europeans and Arabs in Algeria. The *Républicain* published over a hundred articles by Camus, many of which championed social issues such as prisoners' living conditions, immigration, and the plight of workers. As a court reporter, he publicly defended those who were being unjustly persecuted for their beliefs.

Even as Camus's career as a journalist developed, he kept working at other literary efforts. In 1939 he wrote a notable series of eleven articles titled "Poverty in Kabylia," but as a book critic, he reviewed works by Jean-Paul Sartre and others and promoted his own *Noces,* a book of lyrical prose.

All of this activity took place in a highly charged political atmosphere. Britain and France had just declared war on Germany. For their part, the Germans soon conquered Poland with help from the Soviet Union. Camus and Pia took a staunch pacifist position, believing that a peaceful resolution to the conflicts in Europe was still possible. Camus found himself criticized from all sides. His pacifist views were unpopular. Camus also openly condemned the Soviet Union for assisting the Germans in invading Poland, which angered his former Communist colleagues. In addition, the papers Camus worked for were under pressure. Suspected of having anarchist sympathies, the two papers were regularly censored. Eventually the political heat became too great. The *Alger Républicain* folded first, and *Le Soir Républicain* was suspended by decree of the governor-general in January 1940.

THE WAR YEARS

Camus was now unemployed; hoping to take an active stance against Fascism, Camus tried to enlist in the military, but was turned away because of his health. He moved to Oran, where he took a job as a tutor in philosophy and French. Camus had developed a romantic interest in Francine Faure, who lived in Oran with her mother, Fernande, and two older sisters, Christiane and Suzy. The family was protective of Francine and wary of Camus, who was not yet divorced from Simone and was continuing to see other girlfriends, even though he was engaged to Francine. At the same time, Camus worked on the play *Caligula,* the novel *The Stranger,* and *The Myth of*

Sisyphus (an extended essay), envisioning the three works as composing a cycle on the absurd.

Camus did not remain in Oran for long, however. By March 1940 Pia had found work for him in Paris. The Faures disapproved of his leaving Algeria, but he promised to marry Francine if she could join him in France.

Camus arrived in Paris on March 16, where he began work at *Paris-Soir*, a large-circulation newspaper that reflected the politics of the French establishment. The job did not last long, however. By the end of 1940 Camus had been laid off as the paper became more and more a propaganda tool for the Vichy government the Germans had set up after overrunning France. Camus returned to Oran, accompanied by Francine, whom he had married the previous month. The couple settled into life in an apartment next door to Francine's family home.

For Camus, the immediate problem was how to support himself and Francine. Because of his health, Camus was still ineligible for certification as a public schoolteacher. He resorted to private tutoring, but he was able to earn very little. In this situation, Camus had time for writing and to travel frequently to Algiers, where he visited members of his family and friends—including old girlfriends, much to the chagrin of his in-laws. It was at this time that Camus began to outline a new novel, *The Plague*, which would be an allegory of the rapidly spreading evil of Fascism.

In the meantime, Camus's previous works were ready for a publisher—if only one could be found. In April 1941 Pia received Camus's manuscripts for *The Stranger, Caligula,* and *The Myth of Sisyphus.* Much impressed by his friend's works, Pia was determined to get them published in France despite the Nazi occupation and paper shortages caused by the war. Pia circulated the manuscripts to important writers and editors at the Éditions Gallimard publishing house, including Malraux, who had influence over owner Gaston Gallimard, and writer Jean Paulhan.

To stay in business, publishers had to meet with approval from Nazi censors and collaborators. Although Éditions Gallimard circulated the periodical *Nouvelle Revue Française*, with the French Nazi Pierre Drieu La Rochelle in charge, this activity only served as a legitimate front that allowed Éditions Gallimard to publish the works of writers and intellectuals, such as Malraux and Paulhan, who were secretly part of the resistance movement. Impressed by Camus's works, especially *The Stranger*, Malraux and Paulhan convinced Gaston Gallimard to publish the novel and the extended essay, *The Myth of Sisyphus*, simultaneously, as the two works were intended to complement one another.

The Stranger got past the Nazi censors, but Gallimard worried that *The Myth of Sisyphus*, because it included a chapter on the Jewish writer Franz Kafka, would be banned. Eventually, a version of this work was published, but without the Kafka chapter.

Camus, meanwhile, had suffered another relapse of tuberculosis, and his doctor recommended that he recuperate in a high-altitude climate. In July 1942 Camus and Francine went to Le Panelier, a town in the mountainous Vivarais region, in a portion of France the Germans had not yet conquered. Francine stayed through September, then returned to her teaching job in Algeria. In Le Panelier, Camus watched from afar the critical reception of *The Stranger*, including an extensive, mostly positive review by the famous French philosopher Jean-Paul Sartre.

Camus's move to Le Panelier proved to be a mistake. Not only was the high altitude actually bad for someone with tuberculosis, but in November 1942 the Allied forces liberated parts of North Africa from German control while at the same time the Nazis seized the previously unconquered parts of France. Suddenly, Camus and Francine were cut off, caught on opposite sides of enemy lines.

Other than medical treatments in nearby Saint-Etienne and brief trips to Lyons and Paris, Camus stayed in Le Panelier through most of 1943, where he worked on *The Plague*. Meanwhile, Camus kept abreast of his colleagues' activities in the resistance. Pia communicated with Camus, sometimes writing in code, informing him of the activities of Malraux, who was currently in hiding, and Paulhan, who was associating with Nazis and collaborators in Paris and then informing his resistance cohorts of their activities.

This environment of living under and resisting the Nazi occupation, separation, and exile deeply informed the writing of *The Plague*. Critics recognize the plague as an allegorical symbol for the Nazi occupation. Many characters in the novel were composites of Camus himself and his colleagues from the resistance. Biographer Todd suggests, for example, that a local doctor active in the resistance, Roger

Le Forestier, partly inspired the character of Dr. Rieux in the book. Camus fictionalized his own experience in the character of Rambert, the young journalist in the novel who finds himself trapped in a foreign land, separated from the woman he loves.

Camus, like the character he created, at first entertained hopes of escaping his exile and returning home to Francine, and he participated only peripherally in resistance activities. But just as Rambert decides to dedicate himself wholeheartedly in the novel to fighting the plague, Camus moved to Paris in 1943 and actively dedicated himself to the resistance movement.

In his new role as a full member of the resistance, Camus wrote for *Combat*, an underground newsletter published by the movement. Camus also was a part of the underground network responsible for recruiting new members and informing the public of resistance activities.

Working even as a writer for the resistance was dangerous, and Camus could have been imprisoned or killed by the Nazis. Moreover, the always-moving offices of resistance newspapers such as *Combat* were sometimes literally down the street from the headquarters of the German Wehrmacht or French police collaborating with the Nazis. For his part, Camus went beyond writing and printing subversive rhetoric. For example, in one case, he helped a Jewish friend escape Paris, arranging her accommodations with other members of the resistance. Another time he quartered a British officer who was working with the resistance.

Camus's cover for his involvement in *Combat* activities was his job as reviewer of manuscripts at Éditions Gallimard. The publishing house was a Gallimard family enterprise, founded by brothers Gaston and Raymond; their sons and nephews, Pierre, Michel, Claude, and Robert, worked for the company as well. Camus became good friends with most of these family members, particularly Michel and his wife, Janine.

On top of his resistance activities and his cover as editor, Camus continued to work publicly as an author and a playwright. Camus's play *Le Malentendu* was produced in 1944 and featured a young actress named Maria Casarès. The play received mixed reviews, but Casarès was a sensation. Camus was attracted to Casarès, and the two started an affair that was to last intermittently for the rest of Camus's life. The affair was publicly known, and thanks to his association with Casarès and with other celebrities such as the famous French intellectual Sartre, Camus gained notoriety of his own.

As Camus's notoriety grew, rumors of his involvement in the resistance multiplied, naturally increasing the risk of exposure and arrest. Adding to the danger was political discord within the resistance movement itself. An anonymous tract was distributed that publicly accused Camus and Sartre, among others, of only pretending to be in the underground. This action had the dual effect of creating suspicion of Camus among his resistance cohorts and at the same time letting the Nazis know that he was active in the underground. Already suspected of participation in the resistance, Camus briefly went into hiding, but he eventually was able to return to Paris because the Nazis were now more concerned about the advancing Allied forces, which liberated the city in August 1944.

The Paris liberation brought joy to the French. It also proved a boon to Camus's career. General Charles de Gaulle, now the de facto leader of liberated France, banned papers that had collaborated with the Germans and gave official recognition to resistance papers, including *Combat*, whose staff was awarded the Resistance Medal. Pia and Camus were put in charge of *Combat*. Now Camus's work appeared often in *Combat*, and the paper became a forum for publicizing his views. Among his articles was a series on the increasing social tensions in Algeria. Camus also publicly denounced the atomic destruction of the Japanese city of Hiroshima by the United States.

As a journalist, Camus preached a moral responsibility to the truth. In his editorials, he at first supported purges of former collaborators, Fascists, and Nazi sympathizers from public life, and he debated in print with those who advocated mercy for those who had sided with the Germans. Although Camus argued his position fiercely, eventually he came around to a position of moderate tolerance of those on the losing side of the war. Moreover, to drive home his opposition to capital punishment, Camus signed petitions on behalf of collaborators, even though he loathed them.

LIFE AFTER WARTIME

With the end of the war, Camus could at last be reunited with Francine, and she and her family moved to Paris in October 1944. Camus, however, continued his affair with Maria Casarès, at least for a time. But when Camus told Casarès that Francine was pregnant, Casarès ended the affair.

Professionally, too, Camus was caught between opposing forces. He found himself unable to support either the Communists, the most powerful party on the left, or de Gaulle and his more conservative followers. So polarized had French politics become that non-Communist Socialists like Camus were alienated from their intellectual peers on both sides of the political spectrum. Fortunately, Camus's differences with such famous intellectuals as Sartre and Simone de Beauvoir did not keep them from flattering him publicly, so his reputation was largely unaffected.

If he was discomforted by the problem of his political identity, Camus was also struggling with issues of faith. Although a professed nonbeliever in Christianity, he contemplated the battle between good and evil, just as most people of faith did. On one occasion, addressing a group of Dominican monks, Camus said, "I am your Augustine before his conversion. I am debating the problem of evil, and I am not getting past it."[2] This statement probably started the often-argued rumor that Camus was a prospect for conversion to Christianity.

Perhaps more problematic than Christianity for Camus was Communism and his circle of Marxist friends, especially Sartre. Camus now realized that their association with one another caused members of the public to consider him and Sartre to be intellectually linked. Camus claimed not to be influenced by Sartre, nor did he even agree with him on many issues. In Camus's mind, he and Sartre were friends more than they were intellectual colleagues. Indeed, Sartre was just one of many friends with whom Camus could be seen partying in postwar Paris.

By this time, Camus had finished work on *The Plague*, and the novel was published in June 1947 and immediately became a best-seller. Reviews were mostly positive, although the allegorical connections to the Nazi occupation were received with ambivalence by many critics, who felt that portraying a human enemy like the Nazis through a faceless, inhuman symbol like the plague oversimplified the problem presented by human evil. But Camus wanted the symbol of the plague to extend beyond the Nazis. Camus biographer Philip Thody states:

[*The Plague*] . . . protests against the acceptance of this world,
and particularly against what seemed to be taking the place
of Fascism as its supreme incarnation: Stalinist Communism.
. . . An interpretation of [*The Plague*] as an attack on Communist totalitarianism is the best reply to the criticism that its
implicit plea for non-violence makes it an inaccurate allegory
of the Resistance movement.³

Camus's insistence that evil could take the form of either
Fascism or Communism left him politically isolated. He still
sympathized with the Socialists, but as always, Camus could
not agree with any specific political doctrine. He began to
associate with exiled revolutionaries from Spain and Russia,
and he resumed his support for those who were condemned
for ideology, this time targeting known pacifists.

The controversy over his politics did not prevent Camus
from working, however. In 1948 he returned to the theater,
this time with his play *L'Etat de siege* (*The State of Siege*).
The play opened in October 1948, meeting with almost universal contempt from critics. Camus also intended to stage
his previously written *Les Justes;* to avoid another critical disaster, he carefully revised the play, which opened in December 1949. Maria Casarès starred in leading roles in both
plays, and once again she and Camus became lovers. As
with their previous affair, this one was carried on openly.
Not surprisingly, Camus's in-laws were disturbed by the affair, and Francine, forced to witness her husband's unfaith-
fulness, began to show signs of serious depression.

Camus's reputation, however, seemed not to be harmed
either by controversies over his politics or his private life. In
fact, his stature was such that he was able to successfully defend Gaston Gallimard against charges of collaboration with
the Nazis. He also came to the defense of other writers, sign-
ing a petition defending American playwright Henry Miller
against charges of pornography.

At the same time, Camus busied himself with other pro-
jects. During the years 1949 and 1950, Camus regularly
served as editorial adviser for the Gallimards. He was even
given his own imprint, "Espoir," which published the works
of Carl Jung and Federico García Lorca.

Politics were never far in the background for Camus,
however. His controversial essay, *The Rebel* published in late
1951, opened a public rift between Camus and most of the
left-wing intellectuals. The most notable aspect of this
schism was the end of the association between Camus and

Sartre. In the essay, Camus criticized not only Stalinism and Marxism but also generally the revolutionary excesses that led to atrocities following the popular French and Russian Revolutions. Now opponents to Camus lined up on all sides. The right wing already considered Camus an enemy for his earlier radical politics. The left wing felt that Camus had betrayed them by denouncing the Russian Revolution.

Fellow literary figures attacked him as well, including the surrealist André Breton, whose movement Camus had criticized in the essay. Then, in May 1952, critic Francis Jeanson published a review in Sartre's literary journal *Les Temps Modernes* that, among other criticisms, admonished Camus for denouncing the French Revolution and the execution of King Louis XVI. The rhetoric quickly became personal when Camus complained in a response about being lectured by armchair intellectuals who had no real identification with the working class. This response was clearly aimed at Sartre, whom Camus reproached for his bourgeois background and for what Camus considered his minimal participation in the resistance. Jeanson and Sartre responded with scathing articles full of personal attacks. In Sartre's response, the philosopher publicly announced the end of their friendship. Troubled by the controversy his essay had generated, Camus began to feel even more ostracized in Paris's literary circles.

Meanwhile, in his domestic life, Camus watched as his wife suffered from increasingly severe depression. Hoping for an improvement in Francine's condition, the couple went to Oran in 1954, but after Camus and his sister-in-law Christiane Faure had to foil what appeared to be an attempt by Francine to commit suicide, Camus returned to Paris with his wife.

Not long after the couple's return, they separated yet again. Francine was checked into the Saint-Mandé clinic. Electroshock therapy failed to help Francine, and after a second hospitalization she was sent home to Paris, where she was watched constantly by her mother and Christiane. Camus was asked to leave and find housing elsewhere.

At about the same time, politics once again intruded on Camus's life. A group advocating independence for Algeria, the Front for National Liberation (FLN), launched terrorist attacks on Europeans living there. Many leftist French intellectuals supported the FLN, even if doing so meant supporting attacks against civilians, while the right wing demanded strengthened French rule. As in the past, Camus was caught between the left and the right. Camus had long called for fair elections and social equality in Algeria, but he abhorred terrorist action against the working-class Europeans. He also expressed fears that complete independence would relegate Europeans in the former colony to the status of second-class citizens. Because he was Algeria's most famous writer, Camus was recruited to write on the situation there for *L'Express*, publishing his views in thirty-five articles from May 1955 to February 1956; predictably, he was met by scorn from many quarters.

Camus believed some sort of accommodation was possible in Algeria. In January 1956 he traveled to Algiers in an attempt to negotiate a truce. Camus called for a ban on violence against civilians, including the use of torture by the government. The lecture in which he made these proposals was well attended, but Camus's plan was not taken seriously by either side in the conflict, and after visiting with his mother, he returned to Paris. Once again Camus found himself isolated. As biographer Oliver Todd notes, "Camus was seen as a traitor not only to the pied-noirs and the right wing, because he did not sing the praises of French Algeria, but also by the Paris left wing, because he did not support the violence of the FLN."[4] Camus resigned himself to public silence, but privately he wrote to governmental officials, imploring freedom for those who had been jailed for seeking Algerian independence.

Camus returned to his writing. *The Fall*, a novel about sin, guilt, and judgment, was published in May 1956, receiving mixed reviews. Although many considered it a masterpiece, Camus's enemies sought any opportunity to blast him and denounced the book for its obvious autobiographical content. Now living separately from Francine and their children, Camus worked on a collection of novellas titled *The Exile and the Kingdom*. He also returned to professional theater as a director and writer. He adapted and produced William Faulkner's *Requiem for a Nun* and Fyodor Dostoyevsky's *The Possessed*. The plays were performed by a troupe Camus assembled (which included his new lover, Catherine Sellers) and were met with a mixture of admiration, resentment, and confusion on the part of the audiences. Yet despite the controversy over his work, Camus was destined for an immense honor.

THE LATER YEARS

Albert Camus received the Nobel Prize for literature in October 1957. At first, Camus was disinclined to accept this, the greatest of all literary honors, believing that Malraux was more deserving of the award. Gaston Gallimard, who had published so much of Camus's work, forbade a refusal, however. As a result, Camus, Francine, and a number of Gallimards journeyed by rail to Stockholm, Sweden, to attend the awards ceremonies.

Even then, at the pinnacle of his career, Camus could not avoid controversy. During the celebrations an angry young Algerian publicly reproached Camus for his silence on the situation in their homeland. Camus explained that he could not support terrorist violence against innocents, ending with the statement, "I believe in justice, but I shall defend my mother above justice."[5] The French press took his words out of context, representing them not as a statement against terrorist violence, but as a dismissal of independence for Algeria. Camus again found himself scorned, but he was also more famous than ever before, thanks to his new status as a Nobel laureate.

Camus put his prestige to work in his long-standing fight against the death penalty, beginning an aggressive letter-writing campaign to win pardons for men sentenced to death in Algeria and elsewhere. In addition to acting on behalf of condemned Arab nationalists, Camus extended his crusade by writing to authorities in Eastern Europe on behalf of their political prisoners; ultimately, Camus intervened in more than 150 prisoners' cases.

Camus's prestige was not enough to get his views on Algeria's future accepted. His essays and articles about Algeria, collected in *Actuelles I–III*, went largely unread. Camus supported a plan that would grant Algeria partial independence, but there seemed to be an utter lack of interest in this idea. Ironically, French leader Charles de Gaulle, whose right-wing beliefs Camus distrusted, was actually the most receptive listener.

Camus found refuge from the cacophony of his public life in a new family home in the village of Lourmarin, located in the mountainous Vaucluse region of France. Camus, now reunited with Francine and his children, alternated between Lourmarin and Paris. In the peace of this rural environment, Camus spent much of 1959 working on a new novel, *The*

First Man. He was often visited by the poet René Char (for-merly of the resistance movement and now one of Camus's closest friends) as well as Michel and Janine Gallimard.

The Gallimards, their daughter, Anne, and Char visited the Camus family in Lourmarin for New Year's 1960. At the end of the holiday, everyone left to return to Paris; Camus had planned to travel with his family by train, but coaxed by Michel, he decided to ride with the Gallimards in their car instead. It was on January 4, 1960, that the car went out of control, swerving off the road to Paris and slamming into some trees. Albert Camus died instantly; he was forty-six years old. Michel died a few days later from his injuries. Camus's manuscript for *The First Man* was found at the ac-cident site, and his daughter, Catherine, published it decades later. Camus had many times expressed that there is "nothing more absurd than to die in a car accident."[6]

NOTES

1. Oliver Todd, *Albert Camus: A Life*, New York: Knopf, 1997, p. 14.
2. Quoted in Todd, *Albert Camus*, p. 230.
3. Philip Thody, *Albert Camus: 1913–1960*, New York: Macmillan, 1961, pp. 105–106.
4. Todd, *Albert Camus*, p. 339.
5. Quoted in Herbert R. Lottman, *Albert Camus: A Biography*, Gar-den City, NY: Doubleday, 1979, p. 618.
6. Quoted in Todd, *Albert Camus*, p. 413.

CHARACTERS AND PLOT

THE CHARACTERS

Dr. Castel. This doctor, Rieux's older colleague, is one of the secondary characters of the novel. Castel is the first to see the epidemic for what it is about to become. Early in the novel, Castel stands with Rieux against the committee of doctors who are afraid to implement strong measures against the disease. Castel is busy working on serums for most of the narrative, trying to find a cure for the two strains of the plague. Eventually the plague wanes, and Castel's medicine becomes more effective in treating it.

Cottard. No first name is supplied for this character, and he has a fear of the police and civic authorities; the narrative alludes to his criminal past. When the plague seizes Oran, Cottard is singular among the novel's characters in that his life improves, partly because his criminal connections provide profit for him during the quarantine. He insists that he is more content during the quarantine than he was before it. In the allegorical interpretations of *The Plague*, Cottard is usually seen as the collaborator figure who stands with the occupational forces. When the quarantine is finally lifted, Cottard inexplicably fires on a crowd of celebrants and is taken by the police in a bizarre shoot-out, during which he kills a dog.

Joseph Grand. He is a middle-aged man who works as a clerk for the Municipal Office of Oran. Rieux's former patient, he rescues Cottard from suicide early in the novel. As the plague progresses, he silently joins in the effort to combat the epidemic. The harmless and almost anonymous Grand aspires to write a masterpiece novel. As he cannot get beyond the first sentence of his manuscript, he seems doomed to fail in this ambition. Grand is struck with the disease, but he does not die; he is one of the fortunate few who recovers, and his experience marks the beginning of the decline of the epidemic. Suffering from plague fever, Grand orders Rieux to burn his manuscript. By the end of the book, Grand writes a letter to his wife, from whom he is separated, and once again undertakes the writing of his novel.

Michel. This minor character is the concierge of Rieux's building. Part of his job is to remove the dead rats from the premises, and Michel becomes the plague's first victim.

Othon. This secondary character is the police magistrate in Oran. He is a family man—a husband and the father of two children. At one point in the novel he warns Rambert against keeping company with Cottard, a reference to Cottard's criminal past. While Othon is isolated in the quarantine camp, his son dies from the plague despite being injected with Castel's serum. After this episode, Othon dedicates himself to working at the sanitation centers, where family members of plague victims are kept in order to prevent the spread of the disease. Eventually Othon also contracts the plague and dies.

Paneloux. Father Paneloux is described by the narrator as a "learned and militant Jesuit" who is a respected religious authority in the town of Oran. As the plague grows into an epidemic, Paneloux's deep-rooted Christian views begin to clash with the atheistic perspective of Rieux. The priest delivers two important sermons during the disease's siege of the town. In the first sermon, Paneloux characterizes the plague as a weapon sent by God to punish the wicked inhabitants of Oran, who, according to the priest, deserve the infliction because they have been sinful. The priest's second sermon expresses the theme that the plague is the will of God, and even though the citizens of Oran may not understand God's will, they must either accept it or deny it. Finally Paneloux apparently contracts a strain of the plague. The circumstances of his illness are somewhat mysterious—Rieux is not certain that the priest has contracted the plague—and Paneloux dies; his case is recorded as doubtful.

The Prefect. The prefect is the head of the city government of Oran. He initially resists an official public declaration of the plague because he wants to avoid alarming the citizens, but when the deaths mount, he implements stronger restrictions, soon closing off the city and eventually declaring martial law when the epidemic is at its worst.

Raymond Rambert. This young man is a journalist from Paris who is sent to Oran to report on the living conditions of the Arab population in this French settlement. Rambert becomes a victim of circumstance, finding himself unexpectedly trapped in the town once the plague strikes and the quarantine is implemented. Rambert has a fiancée waiting for him in Paris, and the young journalist is driven by an intense anxiety to consider breaching the quarantine (even though that would risk the spread of the epidemic) because he feels that the fulfillment of his love is important beyond all else. Rambert enlists the help of Cottard in the long process of planning an escape from the walled city. During the period of planning, Rambert begins to work for Tarrou's sanitation squads. When Rambert is finally presented with the opportunity for freedom, however, he balks, deciding that his need for personal happiness is outweighed by the necessity of collective action. From that moment he devotes his full-time efforts to combating the plague on the sanitation team. He survives the plague, and at the close of the novel he is finally reunited with the woman he loves.

Dr. Richard. One of the town's highest-ranking doctors, Richard agrees with the prefect in his hesitation to officially declare the epidemic. This minor character is struck with the disease just as the death rate starts to level off.

Dr. Bernard Rieux. Rieux is at the center of the novel. In the final pages, he reveals himself to be the anonymous narrator of the chronicle, which follows the doctor's efforts to fight the plague; along with his allies (including Tarrou, Grand, and Rambert), he seeks to prevent the spread of the epidemic, treating its victims and searching for a cure. Rieux is also one of many characters who suffer from the pain of separation—at the inception of the novel, his wife must leave Oran for a sanatorium located in the mountains in order to recover from a chronic illness. She remains outside Oran for the duration of the quarantine, and Rieux's sole communication with her is through the couple's telegrams to each other. Only after the plague ends does Rieux discover that his wife has died. During the epidemic, Rieux first faces an insensitive bureaucracy, then is overwhelmed by the need to treat terminally ill patients and protect the lives of the healthy, usually by isolating their sick loved ones. He becomes friends with Tarrou, who succumbs to the disease.

Madame Rieux. Madame Rieux comes to stay with her son in order to help support him while his wife is away at the sanatorium. She stays in Oran for the duration of the plague. A silent figure, and one of the only female characters in the novel, Rieux's mother is depicted not only through her son's narrative, but also through Tarrou's diary. She somehow seems to serve as a source of strength and comfort for both men.

Jean Tarrou. Tarrou becomes Rieux's friend during the ordeal of the plague. His diary is an important document for Rieux, who frequently draws from it for observations of life under the plague. Tarrou becomes zealously active in combating the plague, risking his own life to lead a crucial volunteer effort to prevent the spread of the disease. He bonds with Rieux when he tells the doctor that he had been a political activist but came to Oran when he thought that he was helping to spread the same injustice he wished to prevent. Just when the plague finally starts to decline, Tarrou becomes sick and dies, one of its last victims.

The Plot

Part I. The novel begins with a description of the 1940s setting: the town of Oran, a French port located on the Algerian coast. According to the narrator, Oran is an ugly but normal city with unpleasant weather; its people are chiefly interested in commerce, which seems to be the main concern of the whole town. Geographically, Oran is situated on a plateau overlooking a bay. The anonymous narrator, who says he is close to the events he is about to describe, informs the readers that he is playing the part of a historian in order to chronicle these events as an observer.

Then the narrative shifts its focus to Dr. Bernard Rieux, who is worrying about his wife, who is afflicted with a chronic illness, when he begins to notice dead and dying rats in his building and around town. Members of the community begin to feel uneasy about the increasingly high number of dying rats. Rieux discusses the rats with the police magistrate, Othon; the concierge of his building; and with Jean Tarrou, a friend of his neighbors. Later, the doctor declines to be interviewed by a Parisian reporter, Raymond Rambert, on the subject of living conditions of Arabs in Oran. Rieux's mother comes to keep house for the doctor as his wife leaves for a sanatorium to be treated for her illness.

The problem of the dead rats grows out of control, with piles of them forming in the streets and alarming the public. By municipal decree, truckloads are collected and burned, their numbers recorded by the information bureau. After almost two weeks, thousands of rats have been collected. The town is on the verge of panic, but people are informed that the problem has abruptly ended.

On the same day, Rieux is returning to his apartment when he encounters the concierge, who is feeling ill and is leaning on the arm of the town's Jesuit priest, Father Paneloux. The doctor orders him to bed, then is called by a former patient, a clerk at the Municipal Office, wanting him to come check on his neighbor who has suffered an accident. When Rieux arrives, he discovers that the clerk, Joseph Grand, has actually saved his neighbor from hanging himself in a suicide attempt. The neighbor, a mysterious man named Cottard, asks Rieux not to notify the police. Rieux agrees to postpone this action and asks Grand to keep an eye on Cottard. Rieux returns to his apartment, only to find the concierge horribly sick. The concierge dies, becoming the first victim of the plague.

The narrator notes that the concierge's death marks the end of the first period of life under the plague, that of "bewildering portents," and the beginning of a second period that gradually gives way to panic. At this point, the narrator first references Tarrou's diary to supplement his own chronicle. The diary entries include Tarrou's observations of Oran. Tarrou records a conversation between two streetcar conductors in which they discuss a colleague who died of a fever following the disappearance of the dying rats. Tarrou also observes with amusement an old man living across the street, who comes out to his balcony every day after lunch and lures cats on the ground to come close enough for him to spit at them. Tarrou is fascinated by the business-minded populace of Oran and the commercial orientation of the whole town. Tarrou's diary then describes the impressions the dying hordes of rats make on the people of Oran as well as subsequent cases of the fever. This portion of his diary ends with a description of Rieux.

Rieux, meanwhile, isolates the concierge's body and calls another doctor, Richard, the chairman of the medical association. They discuss the outbreak of fever, determining that there have been about twenty cases, and Rieux suggests that Richard should have new cases of the fever isolated, but Richard says that he would need the prefect's order to do so. Rieux then meets Grand and Cottard for the police inquiry into the suicide attempt. Cottard is anxious about the inquiry, still showing fear of dealing with the police. In the next few days, Rieux sees several new cases of the strange fever, most of which result in the patients' deaths. Rieux is visited by an older colleague, Dr. Castel; they discuss the outbreak, and Castel is the first to openly suggest that they are dealing with the plague. The narrator then notes Rieux's reflections on the matter of the plague, drawing an analogy to war, noting the town's reluctance to acknowledge the plague, and contemplating historical outbreaks of the disease.

Grand and Cottard visit Rieux, and together they discuss the rising number of deaths associated with the illness. Grand excuses himself, referring to some mysterious project he must work on. Cottard asks to meet with Rieux later in order to get his advice about an unspecified matter. Rieux agrees, and the two men part. Rieux thinks about Grand, deciding that he is the type of person who would unexpectedly survive the plague. Rieux intuits that Grand is working on a book.

By the next day, Rieux has persuaded the authorities to convene a meeting of the medical association at the prefect's office. The meeting is attended by the prefect, Rieux, Castel, Richard, and several other doctors. Castel insists that they are definitely facing the plague, and Rieux suggests that they implement the extreme prophylactic measures outlined for such an epidemic in the medical code in order to prevent the deaths of half the population. The prefect and Dr. Richard, however, are reluctant to officially declare an outbreak of plague without irrefutable proof, fearing that such an action would cause widespread alarm in the community. The committee decides to enforce the proper measures for dealing with a plague epidemic without the official designation. Leaving the meeting, Rieux observes the grotesque image of a bloody plague victim imploring him for help.

References to the strange illness begin to appear in the local papers, and, making modifications to the severe medical restrictions in order to avoid panic, the authorities discreetly notify the public to take measures to prevent the spread of this "malignant fever." The program includes the extermination of the rats and supervision of the water supply; citizens are advised to practice careful hygiene, report any instances of infection, and consent to the isolation of sick family members.

Rieux meets Grand at his building, and they note the increasing deaths in Oran before turning to the subject of Cottard. Speculating that Cottard has something on his conscience, Grand discusses the odd man's behavior. Later, Rieux meets with the shrewd Castel, who is already undertaking efforts to come up with an antiplague serum.

Thinking about the plague makes Rieux anxious, and he notices his own need for making human contact before the appointment with Cottard that night. In their conversation, the paranoid Cottard expresses suspicion of people taking an interest in him, asking the doctor if the police could arrest a man if he were hospitalized. The conversation ends with Cottard asking about an epidemic, remarking that what the town needs is a big earthquake.

As the deaths increase, Rieux and Castel, who still insists that the epidemic must be a strain of the plague and is researching an effective treatment, implore Richard and the prefect to enforce more stringent measures. On a day when forty deaths are recorded, the prefect issues stronger measures that require mandatory reporting of illness and strict quarantine. The death rate drops briefly, and life in Oran almost returns to normal for a short while, but when the death rate soon rises, the prefect is ordered to declare a state of plague and close the town.

Part II. In the weeks that follow the closing of the city gates, the populace realizes its new condition. No one is allowed to leave. Even phone calls are prohibited because the telephone system is overloaded. Some citizens request that absent family members be allowed to return to the city, but as the death rate rises to hundreds a week, most of these families decide to remain separated, one exception being Madame Castel, who returns from an out-of-town visit to be with her husband. Visitors to Oran, including the young journalist Rambert, suffer an acute despair when they find themselves trapped in a foreign city, separated from their homes and loved ones. The city must immediately cease its considerable trade when its port and gates are closed. The prefect rations food and gasoline, and many shops close; some, however, increase their business as the people try to divert themselves by drinking heavily in the cafés and repeatedly watching the same films in the theaters.

Three weeks after the quarantine is imposed, Rieux is approached by Rambert. The journalist tells him of his desire to return to his fiancée in Paris. Having been told by the prefect that no exceptions can be granted, Rambert hopes that

Rieux will give him a certificate of health. Although sympathetic, the doctor refuses. Annoyed, Rambert leaves the doctor, still determined to escape Oran.

After the first month of the plague, Father Paneloux declares a week of prayer that will be concluded on the next Sunday with a sermon given by the priest. Many people attend the prayer services throughout the week, and on the Sunday of Paneloux's first sermon, the church is overflowing with a huge congregation (which includes Rieux, Tarrou, and Othon). The priest begins his sermon, "Calamity has come on you, my brethren, and, my brethren, you deserved it." The priest then cites the plague of Exodus sent by God as an instrument to punish the wicked. Evoking the wild image of a flail whirling in the air and threshing the world, separating the wheat from the chaff, Paneloux preaches that this plague, too, is God's instrument for separating the just man from the evildoer, punishing those who have not opened their hearts to the love of God. Science cannot help them, he says; the plague is the punishment for their sins. The priest concludes by exhorting his followers to offer Christian prayers of love and to leave their fate in the hands of God. The townspeople have various reactions to the sermon. Some, like Othon, accept the priest's arguments as irrefutable, but others feel they are being punished for an unknown crime. Rieux, on the other hand, is in complete disagreement with Paneloux. The Sunday of the sermon marks the beginning of a period of widespread panic in the town.

A few days later, Grand takes Rieux to his apartment, confiding that his mysterious project is a masterpiece novel. The clerk describes the frustrating artistic process of choosing the words to produce a perfect sentence. Grand shows Rieux his manuscript, but he does not let him read it, instead choosing to read it aloud. The manuscript consists only of the opening phrase of the novel, a sentence that Grand is obsessed by and has endlessly rewritten. As Rieux leaves, he notes the increasing nightly attempts to escape the city, often ending in violence.

Rambert also perseveres in his exhausting efforts to escape the city, first aiming for success through the official channels. After many hours of facing the bureaucracy, he is again told that an exception cannot be made.

Following Father Paneloux's sermon, summer seizes Oran, bringing uncomfortable heat, and the death rate rises to nearly seven hundred deaths a week. In his diary, Tarrou records the growing desperation of life under plague conditions. Tarrou also reacts to the sermon—saying that rhetoric is easy at this early stage—notes a meeting with Rieux, and writes fondly of the doctor's mother.

Tarrou is alarmed to learn from the doctor that the authorities are considering the use of prisoners to help with sanitation efforts against the plague, something to which Tarrou is politically and morally opposed. He offers to enlist a considerable volunteer force for the sanitation effort. Then Tarrou asks the doctor his views on Paneloux's sermon; the atheistic doctor disagrees with the priest's notions of collective punishment, noting that dealing with suffering on a day-to-day basis has given him a different perspective. Tarrou is introduced to the doctor's mother, and the two men leave to go on the doctor's rounds. On the way, Rieux tells Tarrou that he will only have a one-in-three chance of surviving his volunteer sanitation program, but Tarrou says that he is morally compelled to do the dangerous work.

Tarrou immediately organizes the sanitation groups. Their duties are to disinfect houses, to help medical teams quarantine family members and evacuate the infected, and to transport the dead and dying. Tarrou enlists the help of Grand, already overworked from his duties at the Municipal Office, and the clerk acts as secretary for the volunteer teams in his off hours. Some nights, after seemingly endless work, Grand treats Tarrou and Rieux to the latest revisions of the opening phrase to his novel. The exhausted clerk's commitment to the volunteer effort soon begins to interfere with his duties in the city government. The narrator makes the point that Grand embodies the true heroism of the volunteer teams.

During this time, Rambert turns to illegal channels in his attempt to leave the city. Cottard, after overhearing the journalist complain about his situation, approaches the young man on the street. He offers to help Rambert, introducing him to one of his black-market colleagues, Garcia, who in turn agrees to introduce them to another black marketeer, Raoul. Two days later, Cottard and Rambert meet Raoul who names a price for his services.

Rambert meets Raoul the next day at a Spanish restaurant, where he negotiates with a former soccer player named Gonzales. Gonzales plans to connect the young man with two guards, who have been bribed and will provide escape for a fee. Gonzales instructs him to meet him at the cathedral in two days and be prepared to stay with the guards until the right moment. A few days later, Gonzales introduces Rambert to two brothers, Marcel and Louis, the young guards who will help him to escape. The four arrange another meeting. Rambert meets Rieux and Tarrou at the hotel bar for drinks the next night, updating them on his arrangements; he does not respond to Tarrou's invitation to join in the volunteer task force. The next day, Rambert's black-market associates do not show for their meeting. Discouraged, Rambert begins the whole process again, arranging to meet Cottard the next day at Rieux's apartment.

Before Rambert arrives, Cottard converses with Rieux and Tarrou. Cottard declines an invitation to join the sanitation teams. Tarrou confronts him about his fear of the authorities, and Cottard confesses to a criminal past. It is understood that he need not worry about going to jail as long as the authorities are working under emergency conditions. Over the next several days, Cottard and Rambert retrace their trail, and eventually the journalist finds Gonzales. They arrange another meeting, but Rambert is discouraged by the process, believing that it will come to nothing.

Rieux and Tarrou try to cheer up Rambert, but the young man is self-conscious about his desire to escape. He defends his actions, saying that he already fought for a cause on the "losing side" of the Spanish Civil War. His two visitors assure him that there is nothing wrong in his personal quest for happiness. Unable to ignore what Rieux calls common decency, however, the journalist volunteers to help in the sanitation effort until he can escape.

Part III. In mid-August, Oran suffers the plague in its worst phase. Harsh wind and heat increase the misery of the inhabitants. The plague sweeps from the outer districts, striking at the central residential and business districts of the city. Martial law is declared, and patrols and police cordons are set up. After the eleven o'clock curfew, Oran is like a ghost town.

Disposal of the dead becomes speedy and efficient as the number of victims mounts. At first the process is much like an assembly line that starts in the hospital. When the victims die, they are immediately put into readied coffins, then placed in waiting hearses, quickly trucked to the cemetery, given last rites by a priest as they are moved from the hearse, and buried after the most cursory ceremony; if relatives are available to attend, they must hurry because the process takes only fifteen minutes. As deaths increase there is a shortage of coffins and space in the cemetery, so victims are then taken five at a time and the coffins are returned to the hospital for reuse. Careful records are still kept, but soon victims are buried in mass graves, one for men and one for women, and the prefect finally forbids the attendance of family members at the burials. When the plague reaches its most critical point and the victims die in masses, a new streetcar line to the crematorium is opened, and dozens of corpses are transported there at once.

Part IV. Through September and October, the people of Oran become accustomed to living under the plague and have no choice but to "mark time." Monotony and fatigue begin to wear on the residents. Biding his time for the chance to escape, Rambert is in charge of the quarantine station that his hotel has become. Castel, almost ready to test his serum on Othon's plague-stricken son, seems to age quickly from all of his work. Grand continues to show signs of wear under the strain of working in the Municipal Office and for the sanitation teams. Rieux is troubled by thoughts of his own sick wife, and although her telegrams from the sanatorium are optimistic, Rieux discovers through correspondence with the sanatorium doctors that her condition has worsened. Rieux himself feels more isolated when he starts to think that there is nothing he can do for his patients and their families other than bear bad news.

Although he also works under exhausting circumstances, Tarrou seems to hold up under the pressure, and he is fascinated by Cottard, the only person who thrives under the plague conditions. They become friends during this time, and Tarrou writes about the man in his diary. He notes how they spend time together in Tarrou's rare off hours, going into the streets, where Cottard relishes the hedonism of the desperate townspeople there. Tarrou speculates that Cottard is feeling increasingly comfortable—his personality expanding more into social arenas than ever before—now that he is no longer marginalized, alone, but rather equalized with the others; now they are all condemned men.

Rambert makes some progress in his efforts to escape the town. Gonzales finally reconnects him with the two young guards, and Rambert stays in their home, waiting for the signal to flee. At one point, Rieux tells him that he should hurry because Othon has noticed the journalist associating with black marketeers. In the guards' home, their mother questions Rambert about his fiancée and his atheism. Finally, on the night he is supposed to leave, Rambert consults Rieux and Tarrou. They give him the news that Paneloux will take over his volunteer duties and that Castel's serum is to be tested. They are surprised when Rambert announces that he will stay in Oran and devote all of his energy to fighting the plague. Rieux asks him to reconsider, but the young man feels that he cannot be happy as long as the rest of Oran suffers.

At the end of October the serum is tested for the first time, on Othon's young son. Rieux, Tarrou, Rambert, Grand, Castel, and Paneloux gather to observe the young patient's reaction. The results are only partially effective as the boy fights for his life, and the observers can do nothing but watch. The boy's body is wracked by fever, and the distraught Paneloux desperately prays, imploring God to spare the child. But the scientific and religious efforts to save his life are futile, and the child finally dies after his painful struggle. Rieux, deeply affected by the death, launches an attack on Paneloux's original theory that the plague is God's punishment for sin, noting the child's irrefutable innocence. Paneloux's faith seems shaken as he searches for a reason; he decides that God's will must be accepted, even if it cannot be understood. Rieux disagrees, but the two men agree that, despite their differences, they are allies against the plague.

Still troubled by the boy's death, Paneloux announces his second sermon, inviting Rieux to attend. By now, superstition has taken the place of religion for many of the townspeople, and the second sermon is sparsely attended. Paneloux's second sermon emphasizes their collective situation, the priest speaking in a gentler tone and choosing to address the congregation as "we," not "you." He tells them that what he said in the first sermon still holds, but it now needs to be tempered with charity. He says that the trial of the plague ultimately works to the good of Christians, and that the devout must look for that good. The plague teaches needless and needful suffering; the suffering of a child is compensated by eternal bliss. He preaches that this is a time of testing, in which everyone must decide to wholeheartedly accept or deny God's will, even though it is impossible for man to completely understand it.

Paneloux soon tests these views when he is forced to move from his quarters due to the epidemic. He stays with a devout old woman, but then he becomes sick. He refuses to call Rieux, but after watching the priest suffer for some days, the old woman finally calls the doctor. Rieux finds Paneloux's case odd, noting that he does not suffer from many of the symptoms of either strain of the plague. The priest never recovers, however, and dies clutching his crucifix. Rieux records the priest as a "doubtful case."

By autumn, cases of the pneumonic strain of the plague are still on the rise, but the cases of the bubonic strain actually decrease, so the death rate stops climbing. For the first time, a note of optimism emerges, but before the medical association can meet, Dr. Richard dies.

In his diary, Tarrou describes a visit to the municipal stadium, which has been converted into an enormous isolation camp for family members of plague victims. He is accompanied by Rambert and Gonzales, who has been convinced to come along and volunteer in Tarrou's sanitation force.

Rieux and Tarrou take a rare break on a terrace that gives them a good view of Oran. There, Tarrou tells Rieux about his past. His father, a prosecuting attorney, had encouraged Tarrou to take up a career in law, inviting his son to attend a trial. The young Tarrou discovered that he had a moral aversion to the death sentence, and he resented his father for winning what was a capital case. He left home, becoming a political activist involved in attempts to overthrow the established orders in Europe. Soon he realized that his fellow activists were responsible for deaths in the pursuit of their goals, and once again he found himself morally compelled to change his life. At that time, he came to Oran with the knowledge that, figuratively speaking, all men bear the plague. One must therefore take great measures to resist spreading it and playing a hand in any death. The two men then use their medical passes to go to the harbor and enjoy a swim in the ocean. It is an intimate moment that reinforces their friendship bond, now stronger than ever.

By December, Tarrou continues to work hard, Cottard prospers, and Othon is still in quarantine. A bureaucratic error keeps the magistrate isolated even after it is time for him to be released, but when Rambert helps rectify the situation, Othon immediately volunteers to go back to work in the isolation camp. The strain of the situation wears heavily on Grand, who aimlessly wanders the streets. Concerned, Rieux confronts Grand, only to find him sick with the plague.

Rieux and Tarrou make a special exception to the quarantine rules and decide to look after the clerk without evacuating him to the hospital. In his delirium, Grand asks Rieux to look at his manuscript. The doctor finds fifty pages containing only the endless revisions of the same opening phrase, except at the end, which is the beginning of a letter to Grand's estranged wife. Rieux injects Grand with the latest version of Castel's serum, and Tarrou stands watch over him during the night. Although they expect him to die, the clerk begins to recover. Other similar cases indicate that Castel's serum is effective. The death rate finally shows a decrease.

Part V. January sees a rapid decline of the plague. The disease becomes erratic, striking new victims between periods of inactivity. The people of Oran view the situation with cautious optimism, accustomed to the oppression but for the first time thinking about the possibility of life after the disease. Late in the month, a further decline in new plague cases is noticed, and the prefect declares that the measures against the epidemic will be lifted in two weeks.

The narrator notes a change in Tarrou's diary entries. They lack their former objectivity, and the handwriting indicates Tarrou is fatigued. Tarrou, having seen cats for the first time since spring, watches for the man across the street to come out on his balcony and spit at them; when the man does not show, Tarrou speculates that he is either dead or now a recluse. Tarrou also devotes a fond entry to Rieux's mother, impressed by her self-effacement and reminded of his own mother. He then devotes his journal to contemplating Cottard. As the rest of Oran slowly grows more optimistic, Cottard begins to show the consternation he displayed before the plague's onset. He seeks reassurance from his new friends, not wanting the epidemic to end. He holds out hope of being able to start over with a clean slate. Cottard loses his newfound sociability and withdraws into despondency. One day, as they near Cottard's home, Tarrou witnesses two men approach Cottard to question him, at which point the criminal turns and flees. This is Tarrou's last diary entry.

Affected by Oran's new feeling of hopefulness, Rieux returns home the next day expecting a telegram from his wife. His mother informs him that Tarrou has taken ill; Rieux thinks it might be a plague case, but because this is uncertain, Rieux's mother convinces him to treat the sick man there. The doctor soon realizes that Tarrou is infected with both the pneumonic and bubonic strains of the plague, and that there is nothing he can do but wait. Mother and son watch their friend struggle for life; they witness a false remission before Tarrou dies. Rieux cries tears of impotence, contemplates his love for both his mother and his friend, and ultimately sees Tarrou's struggle as the final battle to end a war. He decides that Tarrou is a saint who died in the service of others. The next morning, the hapless doctor receives news that his wife has died in the sanatorium.

On a February morning, the gates of Oran are finally opened, and there is much rejoicing among the townspeople, who are finally free. Ships and trains wait to come into the town, and loved ones are finally reunited, including Rambert, who meets his fiancée at the train station. Lovers soon find themselves enveloped in their own world once again, but for those still separated, some of them parted forever, like the lonely Rieux, the plague is still there. But for the rest of Oran, it is the end of banishment, a massive liberation that inspires people to celebrate and dance in the streets.

It is at this point that Rieux reveals his identity as the narrator, a role he has taken to bear honest witness and provide a true account of the plague. But one person he cannot help is Cottard; Rieux comes across a police cordon on the street where Cottard and Grand live. Cottard has barricaded himself in his home after randomly firing on a group of celebrants in the street, injuring one of them. A bizarre shootout ensues, and Cottard is taken by the police after killing a dog in the street. After the incident, Grand tells the doctor that he plans to make a new start on his novel, as well as his love life, having finally written to his estranged wife. Rieux visits an old asthma patient who tells him that the plague is "just life, no more than that." Rieux goes to the terrace where he recently shared the view with Tarrou. There, he watches the fireworks from the harbor and the jubilation of the people of Oran, who in their strength and innocence seem the same as ever, and Rieux feels at one with them on this level, deciding that there is much to admire in them. He closes by noting that his chronicle is written to describe what must be done in times of pestilence, informing the reader that the plague never really dies but merely hides, biding its time until it can resurface and strike again.

CHAPTER 1

Criticism of
The Plague

READINGS ON
THE PLAGUE

The Limitations of *The Plague*

Gaëtan Picon

The late Gaëtan Picon was one of the foremost
French literary critics of Camus's time. Although he
considers *The Plague* to be an exceptional novel, one
of only a few masterpieces from French literature of
the mid–twentieth century, Picon notes what he per-
ceives to be the novel's weaknesses, including the
troublesome dialogue, macabre pessimism, and especially the limitations of Camus's allegorical representation of the Occupation. Picon asserts that the abstract, inhuman symbol of the plague is not adequate
to the task of representing a human force of evil, as it
was embodied by the Nazi occupation of France. Furthermore, the critic contends that the two levels at
work in the novel, reality and symbol, detract from,
rather than reinforce, one another. Finally, Picon
feels that the novel's pessimism outweighs its pre-
scriptions of personal happiness and resistance.

The Plague has scarcely met with anything but eulogy, and
it would be easy for me to add my plaudits to so unanimous
a criticism. It is all too evident that the novel is important
and of great value. . . . I shall go so far as to say that the un-
reserved praise that Camus's novel has met with is in my
view a questionable homage. To see *The Plague* exclusively
as a subject for eulogies is, I fear, to contrast it with contemporary literary productions from which it is not difficult for
it to stand out. On the other hand, if we consider the novel's
many exceptional and admirable qualities, we are led to
compare it with the greatest works of literature. It is at this
point that it seems to me difficult to remain insensitive to the
book's limits and imperfections.

Some novels are spellbinding and enslave the reader from

Excerpted from Gaëtan Picon, *L'Usage de la techire* (Paris: Mercure de France, 1960).
Translated by Ellen Conroy Kennedy.

the very first moment; others only reveal their power slowly. Obviously *The Plague* belongs in the second category. And Camus intended it to. One must be careful not to find fault with the book for somehow lacking persuasive force. . . . In *The Plague* one should neither look for something stronger and more real than real life nor should one expect the hallucinating presence of an imaginary world that sometimes seems more effective and convincing than reality. Yet how numerous are the books inferior to *The Plague*, in spite of just that ability to shock and that persuasive power! Camus never wanted to ensnare his readers in this fashion. He never intended to play what one might call the "realistic" game, if for the sake of clarity we agree to call "realistic". . . any literary effort whose success is measured by its power to create an illusion. Albert Camus wanted his novel to be first of all a work of art, carefully composed and written, and secondly, an expression of wisdom. The seductions and persuasiveness of realism conceal the writer's art along with the moralist's values: Camus therefore had to limit that portion of illusion which is a necessary part of all novels. If everything remains at a certain distance from us in *The Plague*, if the characters are more than anything else voices in a dialogue, and the events hint of a reality merely suggested, it is because Camus wanted it so. And from this point of view the novel is a success. For at no moment does the story become so obsessive as to make us overlook the dramatic, fervent, bare prose that sustains it, the moral maxims that mark its course. Nor do we ever lose the sense of an art which blends conflicting riches, an order born of disorder, that is never so striking as in the book's many and characteristic transitions: the transition from the pure and simple narrative (*récit*) to the chronicle, from realism to allegory, from the individual perspective to the collective perspective, from spareness to lyricism, from the dramatic to the humorous.

Two Registers: Reality and Symbol

The Plague is one of those books which far from confining us to the outer appearances which it builds up around us attempts rather to free us from these appearances. This it does by keeping the apparent within a perspective such that we suspect it is not sufficient unto itself. It is one of those books which represents more than it presents, which consists less in what it gives than in what it conceals. To simplify things, one can say that *The Plague* is an allegorical novel. The quotation from DeFoe at the very beginning of the book is a first proof of this allegorical intention: "It is as reasonable to represent one kind of imprisonment by another as it is to represent anything that really exists by that which exists not." Very soon, we know without any doubt what significance to give to the allegory. The epidemic of the plague which breaks out in Oran in the 1940's is very plainly the symbol of a historical reality which we know only too well. How can one fail to recognize this city, taken by surprise by the abrupt apparition of tragedy, a city soon its own prisoner, no longer able to communicate with the free world except through memory, imagination and the vaguest of messages; a city shut in upon a universe of exile and separation, of suffering and brotherhood; a people of whom it is said that "a number of them piled into the maw of a crematory, evaporated into oily fumes, while the rest, chained down by fear and impotence awaited their turn." But if this city fallen prey to the plague evokes wartime France under the German occupation, it is also any human city struck by any of the thousand plagues that destiny reserves for us. It gives us an image of that human condition for which Pascal long ago said that imprisonment was the best symbol. The importance of the book stems from the fact that it unites a metaphysical message whose sense soon becomes apparent with the specific emotional state that arises from its historical reference.

The story of the plague at Oran is not presented as a legend, but as a true story, as an historical fiction, if one may call it such. Consequently, how can it totally avoid the basic exigencies of truth? Actually the author presents his story both as reality and as symbol, as *Dichtung* (poetry) and *Wahrheit* (truth). From this stems the alliance, or more precisely, the juxtaposition of the symbolical and the realistic. Sometimes the author sought the immediate shock, the illusive power of realism: for example, when he evokes the apparition of the dead rats in the houses and streets of the city; Dr. Rieux's separation from his wife; the death agony of Judge Othon's son; the panic that ends a presentation of Gluck's *Orpheus and Eurydice* when the plague overwhelms a singer on the stage. In contrast, the pages written in chronicle style inform us of the events indirectly by means of the narrator's reflections about them, rather than directly. They give an impression of material distance: the narrator interposes himself between us and the events, and judges them after they have happened; also of spiritual distance: the plot seems to take on perspective, achieving a symbolical character.

I do not reproach the book for the contrast between these two "registers"; the transitions from one to the other are effected remarkably well. But I think that the division of the work into these two levels, and these two tones, keeps it from reaching its full stature in either direction, and is an obstacle to the attainment of that living and formal unity which alone could move us and satisfy us completely. The allegorical elements break the latent power of the real, and the reality dissipates the legendary aura as it forms. Thus, *The Plague* is neither deeply rooted in the real stuff of life nor in the poetical matter of myth. Allegory leaves reality too small a chance to catch us in its net—and the realistic elements lend allegory merely the value of an intellectual gesture. Thus, at every moment, and in whatever way one looks at it, the novel is paralyzed by its own form. Of all our contemporary writers, Camus was without doubt the most anxious to achieve the mythic; but the incapacity of allegory to become myth in *The Plague* is evident and reveals perhaps the real source of Camus's failure. One need only think of Kafka's *The Trial*, Melville's *Benito Cereno*, or Hawthorne's *The Scarlet Letter* to measure the distance that separates *The Plague* from those few mythic novels truly animated by a sense of the poetic.

WHAT'S WRONG WITH *THE PLAGUE*

On another level, the dialogues are troublesome in the same way. It is plain that their "register" is one of intellectual stylization. The voices answer one another like voices in a play-reading, when, unmindful of décor and characters, we are attentive only to the alternating brilliance of the language. But Camus seems suddenly to remember that his characters are not eloquent abstractions, and to want to remind us of their deep involvement in the tragic reality of the plague-ridden city. He then separates the voices and introduces moments of dramatic orchestration into these short silences. But the voices tend to come together again, and the orchestrations seem artificial. Plague-ridden Oran does not manage to live in these dialogues. . . . And very often the sentences which separate the voices and the dialogue seem like so much dramatic padding:

"Who taught you all this, doctor?"
The answer came promptly:
"Suffering."

or

"Do you really imagine you know everything about life?"
The answer came through the darkness, in the same cool,
confident tone.
"Yes."[1]

It is tempting to see in Albert Camus a great writer who
has not managed to discover where to apply his efforts. Neither the story, the novel, nor the theater have thus far provided him a medium that measures up to his gifts. A moralist in the tradition of the seventeenth century, or perhaps
one of those sagacious travelers who flourished in the nine-
teenth century, he is face to face with a literature divided
into definite genres which challenge the writer to prove definitely his worth in one of them. Perhaps the hesitation one
senses in Camus's . . . work, which tends simultaneously toward . . . the gestures of melodrama, and the spareness of
abstraction is the sign of a wealth of possibilities. Or is it
rather a certain shortness of breath, which, lacking the
power to make a single torch flame high, kindles many
smaller fires at one and the same time? The same ambiguity is implicit in Camus's very style, a style whose peerless
qualities we immediately recognize but whose inner division often has a paralyzing effect. Torn between reality and
myth, Camus is also torn between a classical spareness of
style, continually and admirably exemplified in his writing,
and the lyrical and dramatic impulse which is also deeply
his. I believe that his two stylistic veins extinguish each
other more often than they nourish each other, when they
are mixed together. I prefer in Camus either the extreme of
classical spareness—as in the apparition of the rats or
Rieux's separation from his wife in *The Plague*—or those
pages in which Camus gives full expression to an interior
lyricism, as he does in *Noces* (Nuptials), "The Minotaur," or
"Prometheus in Hell." When Camus follows his bent and expresses himself in images, his lyricism, in spite of his dis-
trust of the poetic, is surprisingly effective. In *The Plague* this
lyricism often seems ashamed to show itself, strangling itself with its own hands, so to speak, as soon as it becomes

1. *The Plague*, trans. Gilbert Stuart (New York: Alfred A. Knopf, Inc., 1948), pp. 118, 119.

conscious. It is there nonetheless, but we feel an inner constraint and a tendency to replace images with an abstract rhetoric rather than a reaching toward the poetic: "The spiteful winds of the sky," "the waters of the plague," "the panting night."

A will to impose order and unity in conflict with deep inner tensions, in the form of his work as well as in its meaning, such is Albert Camus as he appears to us. And we like him because of the battle he wages with himself, and not for the victory or the defeat that ends it. For the artistic balance and the moral wisdom he offers us betray the passionate ardor from which they spring, bringing us peace where we expected fervor.

With Camus there is always a surge upward and wings stopped in mid-flight. And it is here that this wisdom reaches its deepest expression, one might say—and I would add, its most irremediable expression, because it is a wisdom which knows what it opposes. It need not fear that one day it will discover its opponent and find itself unprepared. Camus knows what disturbs him, but he does not wish to be disturbed. Violence is at the source—calm has the last word. This is clearly manifest in the manner he has of triumphing over the absurd. He knows the bite of the absurd, but its violence in him is not so strong that he cannot escape it, or that he has no recourse but some other form of violence. To the intensity of the absurd, Camus opposes, not the intensity of human values, the passion for man and his actions, but the wise consciousness that it is impossible to live in the absurd and that values really do exist. This explains the quite rational way in which he moves. . . . Camus moves through reflection and reasoning from the absurd to the sense of value. Living is not enough for him; he must think. And doubtless he must think in order to be able to live. . . . Camus affirms that one must not act in terms of *ivresses* (intoxication), but in terms of thought. And what attitudes have a value to set against the absurd? Revolt, answers Camus. But the term is equivocal, as is clearly apparent when one reads *The Plague* after *The Myth of Sisyphus*. Revolt in *The Plague* has lost its Promethean halo; far from justifying man's triumphant undertakings, it merely nourishes his desire for protection. This is a defensive and not an offensive position. What Camus really retains from the notion of revolt is that there exists one part of man which does not tolerate humiliation. What shall we do for the sake of dignity? That is above all what we should like to know.

THIS CANNOT BE ENOUGH

To Camus, who started with a total and unqualified demand it now seems to be enough that, in the long run, suffering and injustice be spared man, and that man's right to achieve happiness be respected. Does this not seem a rather modest request? When Camus declares that heroism ranks below the will to be happy, doubtless one is tempted to agree with him. It would still be necessary for happiness to put us in touch with some supreme force, to be a positive and passionate affirmation. But it seems to me that Camus never gives anything but a negative definition of happiness. If happiness consists merely in escaping from the plague, this cannot be enough. We want happiness to be the possibility of reaching something outside the realm of the plague, we want to find in it a use and justification of our freedom. That one must fight against the plagues that enslave man: this is the sole conclusion which, according to Albert Camus, is not open to doubt. But it can only be the first principle of morality; the essential thing we must discover is what we should do with the liberty rescued from plagues.

It is not enough to protect man from scourges. Still less is it enough to feel one might be exempt from reproach simply by virtue of not being on the side of scourges. One character in *The Plague*, Tarrou, thinks that our only moral duty, or rather our unique moral possibility, is not to be oneself a carrier of germs. It is true that for Dr. Rieux morality is first of all a question of curing people. But the two men share the same basic moral attitude, certainly not a passive one, since they both fight and sacrifice themselves to the same degree—Tarrou just as much as Rieux, more than Rieux even, since he pays the sacrifice. But it is basically a defensive attitude, and at bottom, an attitude of nonintervention. There are wounds to dress, crimes to understand and forgive: this is the sum of what one can do. Medicine and understanding: this is the ethic proposed.

And this is certainly the only ethic which is free from danger, the only one which leaves us with perfectly clean hands, which frees us of all responsibility in catastrophes. But the insufficiency and the inefficacity of any attitude is defined precisely by the fact that it holds no dangers. How can one fail to recognize and admit this is Camus's major obsession? But how can one not want to go beyond it? When we fear that our will to obtain something better may lead to something worse, refusing to intervene because we are concerned about future consequences, content to look after the victims so as not to add to the scourges, we shirk what has been the mission of certain men destined to bring us examples and revelation, and we exchange risk for security, responsibility for peace.

The notion of risk does not exist in *The Plague.* Everything happens as if the author were seeking to confine himself to a wisdom so sure that it contains no element he might be apprehensive about. And with the notion of risk goes the notion of choice. For in the last analysis, who can fail to see that his duty is to fight against the plague, and if he is a doctor, to do his job? The plague is an indisputable scourge, which leaves no room for hesitation. A natural catastrophe, it does not call forth any human justification, and there is nothing to risk in combatting it except one's life. But there are other scourges. Those which come from the will of men—war, social oppression, spiritual oppression—these are more ambiguous. Here, in order to take sides, we obviously need values other than those of defense and nonintervention, and, in order to vanquish, much more powerful forces. Certainly nonintervention is better than intervention that is criminal. But when the time comes to repel and challenge murderous passions, the tranquil commitment to nonviolence is ineffectual: it is as inoperative in the realm of value as it is as a weapon in the realm of force. If we are to make humiliation and suffering lose face, rather than merely to denounce them, we must show what meaning may be given to a human life freed from pain and humiliation. And we shall not crush our monsters in the name of an understanding that would transform us into accomplices, but in the name of some more powerful passion. In the voice of the author of *The Plague* one comes upon more than an echo of the great rationalist voices of the past: precisely those which failed to forestall the tragic events of our time. But in art as in existence, what is baffling to wisdom may not be so to the passions.

The Plague's Allegorical Nature Is Key to the Novel's Power

Germaine Brée

Germaine Brée is a literary scholar who specializes in Albert Camus and is one of the most important and respected critics of his work. Having lived in Algeria, she was a contemporary of Camus and knew him personally. Since Camus's death in 1960, Brée has written, edited, and otherwise participated in the publication of many volumes on the subject of his body of work.

In this excerpt from the revised edition of her book, *Camus*, Brée explores the significance of the symbolism of the plague, responding to those critics who view *The Plague* as a flawed and limited allegory. Contrary to those critics, she suggests that had Camus chosen to depict a human enemy (instead of the plague) as the symbol of evil, then he would not have been able to develop the additional levels of meaning in the novel. Brée believes that these deeper themes of the novel are developed through the positioning of the various characters in relation to the inhuman, faceless symbol of the plague. In Brée's interpretation, the symbolism of the plague is the key to significance in the novel because it is closely interconnected to the characters and themes, and this process of interaction between these elements further increases the significance of the symbol.

From the same human indifference of *L'Etranger*, the plague, as it envelops Oran, draws its pestilential power. Perhaps that is why Camus chose that particular symbol of evil. The people of Oran, as Dr. Rieux describes them, have little sense of reality, of either good or evil, and this allows the plague to make rapid progress among them. Unopposed, it organizes all that is bad in human life into a coherent and independent system: pain, death, separation, fear, and solitude. And it disorganizes and destroys all that is good: freedom, hope, and most particularly love. The people of Oran are easily led to accept the plague as the very form of reality. It does not develop as would any living organism, it spreads, monotonous, rigid, inhuman, occupying a city which, because of its lack of awareness, is already conquered.

The plague is not the symbol of an outer abstract evil; it merely applies and carries to their logical limits the values implicit in the unconscious attitudes of the citizens of Oran. It is monstrous, monstrous as the acts of destruction into which in this twentieth century we have all been collectively plunged: war, mass repressions, concentration camps, evils all seemingly produced without our participation, the result of some invisible all-powerful mechanism. Had Camus merely chosen a group of human beings as the symbol of this evil of our times, the deeper intent of his novel would have been lost.

It was in the little-known book of essays, *Le Théâtre et son double,* by the rather esoteric writer Antonin Artaud that Camus found the ancient symbol of the plague used in a manner which suited the theme he was pondering. It suggested the double symbolism which had satisfied him aesthetically in Melville's works, especially *Moby Dick,* one of his favorite books. For Artaud, the plague is the concrete equivalent of a spiritual illness, both an individual and a collective illness. After quoting at length from chronicles which describe the pestilence, Artaud concludes: "Thus the plague seems to show up in certain places, preferring all the parts of the body, all the sites in physical space *in which human will and conscience and thought are close by and likely to manifest themselves. . . .* If we are willing to accept this spiritual image of the plague, we shall consider the physical disturbances manifested by the victim of the plague as the concrete and material form of a disorder equal, on other levels, to conflicts, struggles, cataclysm and collapse all brought about by events. . . . *And . . . we can agree that external events, political conflicts, natural disasters . . . are shot into the onlooker's sensitivity with the force of an epidemic.*" [*"Le Théâtre et son double"* (1944 Gallimard edition), pp. 22–26 (my italics)]. From whatever point of view we consider it—individual, political, social, metaphysical—the symbol of the pestilence thus used establishes a direct connection between evil and a paralysis of our human conscience, intelligence, and will.

In spite of abundant documentation, it did not prove easy for Camus to draw from this ambiguous symbol, powerful though it may be, the novel he wished to write. It was not so much the general collective movement of the plague that caused the difficulties—its appearance, its short tussle with a somnolent and abstract administration unable to cope with so concrete an evil, its metamorphosis from invader into an omnipresent form of government—but how to create characters who, taking position in relation to the plague, could carry the main themes of the novel and give to it the deeper significance of the symbol.

In the Notebooks, Dr. Rieux and Father Paneloux, Tarrou, Grand, Cottard, and last of all Rambert, slowly emerge after the main themes have been stated: they are voices and attitudes before they are individuals, yet each one is clearly differentiated by the particular form of sensitivity his suffering reveals. In the background is the silent figure of Mme. Rieux, the doctor's mother. In his notes Camus attaches a greater importance to her presence than her role in the novel seems to warrant, but she is closely linked to his main characters through whose eyes we follow the story, that is, to her son Dr. Rieux and to his friend Tarrou, over whom she exercises a strong attraction. These three characters are at the heart of the novel. Mme. Rieux's fragile presence beside her son throughout the epidemic and at Tarrou's bedside at the hour of his death is far more indomitable in its serenity than the baroque autocracy of the epidemic itself. It is through her that Camus introduces a human perspective essential to his novel which none of his other characters convey to us in quite the same way.

COMING TO TERMS WITH REALITY

Of all the characters in this novel Dr. Rieux is, in a sense, the least complicated. He has devoted his life to fighting illness and death; the pestilence is only an acute manifestation of his daily enemy, man's mortality. Rieux knows the hopelessness of his undertaking and the epidemic only emphasizes it: as a doctor he can diagnose, not cure. What normally he can bring to his fellow men—hope and temporary alleviation from pain—the plague snatches from him. His ethics are clear: a doctor fights illness, and to fight an illness one must first recognize what that illness is. Like his friend, Dr. Castel, he quickly realizes the full implications of the situation in which the city of Oran finds itself and, with no illusions, he does to the limit of his strength what it is his function to do. He is one of two or three men who realize at once that the nature of the evil appearing in Oran is unusual and must be fought by new methods. He looks on the scene with the same unwavering eyes as does his mother. But in the meantime his own wife, sick of tuberculosis, dies in a sanatorium, alone and removed from the scene of his struggle. When she leaves for the sanatorium at the beginning of the book we sense that, even before the advent of the plague, Rieux has allowed one dimension of life to slip from his hands, that is, the personal, total love that links two human beings. He survives the plague, but alone, dehumanized. As he watches the exuberant crowd on the night when the gates of Oran finally open, he realizes that he will always be a prisoner of the plague. For him the plague is, in essence, the clear inner awareness of man's accidental and transitory presence on the earth, an awareness that is the source of all metaphysical torment, a torment which in Camus's eyes is one of the characteristics of our time.

Tarrou lives this anguish in a more concrete way. He is far more preoccupied than Rieux by the material, visible substance of the world. It is from Tarrou's notebooks that we get the sensuous and physical description of both the city and its inhabitants, and a sense of the changes that take place in the moods, rhythms, and outer appearance of Oran. His own inner adventure had begun long before his arrival in Oran. It began when Tarrou realized (like young Albert Camus) that men condemn other men to death; the judge, in this instance, had been Tarrou's father and the shock of the revelation threw Tarrou out of his normal human orbit. He left his home, the father he could no longer tolerate, the mother he loved. He broke all ties with a society he condemned for coldly killing men in the name of justice. He now felt he could not ever judge his fellow men. When seeking to act in revolutionary political causes in favor of social reform, he found this form of action made him once again a witness to the execution of a human being in the name of justice. Tarrou then comes to the realization that no doctrine is worth killing for: "my affair," he says, "was that hole in the chest" of the man shot down. When he settled in Oran before the advent of the plague Tarrou withdrew from all action, apparently seeking through observation and meditation a road toward the selfless purity of the saint; he wanted no part in any evil. During the plague he becomes the animating spirit of the volunteer teams fighting the pestilence which in the end takes his own life.

Unlike Rieux, Tarrou cannot come to terms with the reality of man's metaphysical condition nor accept man's participation in its cruel rites. He is touched more deeply perhaps than Rieux at the very source of life, in his sensitivity. He experiences the compassion we see in Mme. Rieux's eyes but not the intellectual serenity that accompanies it. In his notebooks Tarrou carefully records the actions of two old men whom he observes: the first automatically appears every day at the balcony of his room, wheedles the cats in the courtyard into coming under his windows and then, when they do, energetically spits on them; the second old man, an asthmatic patient of Dr. Rieux's, spends his time in bed, a veritable hourglass of a man, who transfers chick-peas one by one from one receptacle to another. The life of the first man is entirely disrupted by the plague, since the cats disappear; the second triumphantly and imperturbably survives. These two men, in a mechanical, unconscious way, are crude replicas of Tarrou and Rieux. In his essential absurdity, the first needs to establish a relation with a living being; the second reduces life to the most elementary and indifferent automatism. Tarrou wonders whether this second man is a saint, and we realize that what distinguishes Tarrou from Dr. Rieux is that Tarrou is trying to purge himself of all evil, trying to transcend his human condition.

Upon Rieux and Tarrou, Camus puts the burden of a full awareness of the nature and significance of the plague; but to them he also gives the one rich moment of escape from the pestilence. Leaving the plague-ridden city behind them one night, Rieux and Tarrou take a long swim in the sea. The human nightmare is dissipated and the joy and beauty of life flood their entire beings as they move side by side in the buoyant waters. For a few moments they emerge into the greater cosmos of sea and night, freed from their obsession with human suffering and the prison walls the plague has built around them. For Rieux and Tarrou, the plague is first and foremost a certain metaphysical and intellectual view of life, a part of themselves which, if it goes unchallenged, will dominate and kill the sense of oneness with others, the feeling of harmony with the earth, the physical freedom and enjoyment which are life itself.

CONCERNED WITH LIVING (LOVE AND HAPPINESS)

Rambert and Grand, both allies of Rieux and Tarrou in the fight against the pestilence, are less involved intellectually. Rambert, the journalist, is concerned not with understanding but with living. Physically sturdy and characteristically generous, he discovered before coming to Oran that the only remedy against human anguish is love and the happiness it brings. For ideologies he has no use. Having fought in the Spanish civil war, he knows how murderous heroism can be even in the best of causes. He is in Oran by accident, on a special assignment—reminiscent of one of Camus's own a few years earlier—and he has no sense of belonging to the city. The woman he loves is in Europe and all he wants is to join her there. More than either Rieux or Tarrou he carries the fundamental theme of the book: the suffering the plague causes by separating and isolating all who—consciously or not—love each other. Whether the separation is temporary, as in the case of Rambert, or final, as in the case of Judge Othon and his son, it kills hope and joy, the sense of duration, faith in the future, the value of human life. Rambert's efforts to flee the closed city prove useless, but it becomes clear to him that he who values happiness cannot allow the plague to reign around him. When, on the station platform at the end of the book, Rambert opens his arms to the slim figure of the woman he loves, he is, in contrast with Rieux, one with the crowd around him. For all these individuals separately, life is in essense what the plague destroys, that is, the freedom to love as though both love and lovers were eternal: "They now knew that if there is any one thing that one can always wish for and sometimes get, it is the tenderness of human beings."

Grand had lost the love that is precious to Rambert, for he had let it be stifled by the dreary routines of his insignificant life as clerk in the city administration. In its stead he has undertaken to write a perfect novel; although after many years of work he has not been able to formulate to his own satisfaction the first and only extant sentence, he dreams that eventually his book will make editors stand up and cry "Hats off, gentlemen!" It is his form of rebellion against the bureau-cratic pettiness of his life. The plague merely accentuates all the routines and servitudes with which Grand deals, for it is his role to keep the endless files and records that Rieux needs, and Grand does this unquestioningly: "The plague is here, ob-viously . . . we must defend ourselves. Ah, if only everything were as simple." Grand eventually falls sick of the plague and then recovers; but he burns the sheets and sheets of paper covered with successive versions of his one and only sen-tence. What he finds alive again in his heart is the memory of Jeanne, the wife whom he loved and had lost.

Grand and Rambert, who come out of the plague with a greater degree of humanity than before, are the most touch-ing figures in the novel. Rieux, Tarrou, Rambert, and Grand all fight the plague for different reasons but essentially be-cause each in his way is already, as Tarrou admits, plague-stricken, accustomed to living with the plague and to deal-ing with it more or less consciously but honestly in his private life.

A DIFFERENT ROLE: PANELOUX AND COTTARD

In the lives of Father Paneloux and Cottard, however, the plague plays a very different role. At the beginning of the book, when Rieux begins to organize his medical service, the church also prepares to bring its consolations to the cit-izens of Oran. Father Paneloux preaches a first sermon [This sermon recalls some of the exhortations made in 1940, which called on France to consider the defeat and occupa-tion as the natural punishment for its sins and to accept it therefore as such, to repent and trust in God; it also recalls the exhortations of the prophets calling upon the children of Israel to repent in the midst of the disasters that struck them.] in front of a crowded audience. He develops tradi-tional Christian themes: the people of Oran have sinned and God is striking them as he struck the people of Egypt. The trials they suffer are a purification, gratefully to be accepted, for they will lead to a reconciliation with God in this or the next world: "My brothers, you have fallen into misfortune; my brothers, you deserved it." When Paneloux joins the team of voluntary workers it is because, like Rieux, he con-siders it his duty to tend those that suffer. But his mental at-titude toward the plague is entirely different from that of Rieux. In his eyes human suffering is willed by God and justified by man's guilt. The plague poses no new problem for him until that moment when he witnesses the long and excruciating agony of a little boy, the son of Judge Othon. After that experience he can no longer justify the ravages of the plague, and he withdraws into a somber meditation out of which emerges a second tragic sermon. Bowing to the mystery of God's will, like Christ at Gethsemane, Paneloux takes upon himself the ills of the earth and, reliving the Passion, dies alone, consciously draining to its dregs the same cup of suffering as Christ's, accepting that God's will be done.

Heroic though he be, Father Paneloux is the only person with whom Dr. Rieux in his humanity comes to no understanding, though Paneloux, too, abandons the attempt to understand: "My brothers, the moment has come. We must believe all or deny all. And who, among you, would dare to deny all?" Unwilling to deny his God, he accepts what he takes to be God's will in its totality. If we judge by his death, he has given a negative answer to the question he had been debating in an unpublished treatise: "Can a priest consult a doctor?" But the conclusions the two men draw from their encounter with the plague are irreconcilable: for Rieux, a doctor cannot accept consolation from a priest; for Paneloux, a priest cannot accept the ministrations of a doctor, since the doctor is the enemy of a God who permits evil to reign in this world. "Since the order of the world is governed by death," Rieux says, "it is better perhaps for God that one should not believe in Him and should fight with all one's strength against death."

Cottard is an ambiguous character. A criminal, he is at ease in pestilence-ridden Oran where death threatens everyone and where, as a consequence, he enjoys a reprieve. Upon him Camus accumulates every form of violent death—except death by the plague: Cottard is a condemned man; he first attempts to commit suicide and then, shooting wildly at all who approach him, he is finally shot down by the police to whom he refuses to surrender. Whatever his crime may have been, he wanted above all to escape from its consequences: he prefers suicide to judgment. While the plague was rampant, he strove to build up a solid front of respectability. Tarrou immediately understands Cottard's latent anxiety and his complicity with the Oran plague, which frees him from that other form of evil, man's brutal justice. The plague at least leaves Cottard with a chance, a loophole of hope for the future, which is all he needs. There is something quite pathetic about Cottard's blind attempts to acquire respectability, his angry discussion of the trial of Meursault—an account of which he reads in the papers—and his irritated denial of the statistics which show that the power of the plague is receding and that, consequently, his own reprieve is at an end. Some critics have thought of Cottard as the embodiment of evil itself, a somewhat questionable interpretation, perhaps, given the anxious humanity of the little man himself. Unlike Rambert, the journalist, who seeks to escape from the oppressive atmosphere of the plague into normal living, Cottard finds refuge from the consequences of his past life in the stifling oppressiveness of Oran.

THE STIFLING ATMOSPHERE

It is essentially that stifling atmosphere which Camus sought to convey: "I wish to express, by means of the plague, the feeling of suffocation from which we all suffered and the atmosphere of threat and exile in which we lived. At the same time I want to extend my interpretation to the notion of existence in general. . . . The plague will give an image of those whose share during the war was meditation, silence, and moral suffering." The plague, therefore, in whatever context we consider it, symbolizes any force which systematically cuts human beings off from the living breath of life: the physical joy of moving freely on this earth, the inner joy of love, the freedom to plan our tomorrows. In a very general way it is death and, in human terms, all that enters into complicity with death: metaphysical or political systems, bureaucratic abstractions, and even Tarrou's and Paneloux's efforts to transcend their humanity. In the fight against the plague there are neither heroes nor victories, there are merely men who, like Dr. Rieux and Grand, refuse to submit to evidence. However useless their actions, however insignificant, they continue to perform them. It matters little for what reason so long as they testify to man's allegiance to men and not to abstractions or absolutes.

The main characters do not alone carry the full power of this theme; it is woven into the substance of the novel as Rieux describes the effects of the plague on the inhabitants of Oran: lovers and families separated in life and in death, "immigrants" thrown out of the stream of human feeling by the plague, passive collaborators "exiled" upon the arid shores of a collective fate. To consider the main characters of *La Peste* apart from the collective life of Oran is to mutilate them; if we examine them only in relation to the fate meted out, a little too neatly perhaps, the novel loses an essential dimension and becomes more nearly an allegory. Considered in its totality the novel transmits a personal experience lived in depth and which Camus could express in no other way. Camus spoke of the novel as a confession; Dr. Rieux speaks of his chronicle as a testimony. The confession takes us back directly to Camus's main preoccupation: his need to rethink the fundamental problems of life. The war years had apparently brought the massive evidence of what Camus, in *Le Mythe de Sisyphe,* had set out to deny: the insignificance of the individual human being, the absurdity of human aspirations. That these years almost succeeded in plunging Camus into silence and despair, *La Peste* is there to prove. Nowhere has Camus more starkly depicted his reaction to the total unintelligibility of man's condition, nor his protestation against the amount of suffering inflicted on human bodies and human feelings. No religion, no ideology, he tells us, can justify the spectacle of the collective suffering inflicted upon man. Our minds waver, and Tarrou and Paneloux both die.

In this context *La Peste* marks a change in emphasis; leaving the universe to itself, Camus turns to men. And here the testimony begins. Against all the intellectual evidence in the world stands man with his indomitable needs, his love of life, his will to live. Camus observes him with confidence and this in spite of man's indifference to what he represents, in spite of his depreciation of what he most values, in spite of the facility with which he enters into complicity with the plague. It would have been difficult for Camus to express directly what he felt so deeply within him: the compassion for human beings, the respect for man's fragile joys. Neither sentimental nor blind, his humanism would have been meaningless had he attempted to abstract it from the experience that nourished it. This is why *La Peste* is, within its limits, a great novel, the most disturbing, most moving novel yet to have come out of the chaos of the mid-century.

CHAPTER 2

Meaning in *The Plague:* Theme and Symbol

Levels of Meaning in *The Plague*

John Cruickshank

British critic John Cruickshank has influenced decades of scholarship on the work of Camus. In the following viewpoint, Cruickshank identifies three main levels of significance in the novel: first, the literal level documents the Oran community's struggle against the disease; the second level is the famous allegorical dimension which parallels the Nazi occupation of France during World War II and extends to tyrannies in general; finally, the third level of meaning is the universal application, dealing with the evil of suffering inherent in the human condition. These three levels of the novel have become standard in Camus discourse since Cruickshank delineated them over forty years ago, and many other scholars have incorporated them into their own discussions.

Cruickshank classifies *The Plague*—which he refers to by its French title, *La Peste*—as a symbolist novel, which he defines as a work having two or more levels of significance that are fused into an organic whole that is more complete than a mere allegory. Cruickshank also provides an analysis of form and technique, examining the novel from the perspective of Camus's ideal of fiction—as established by the French author's own literary scholarship.

A myth, for Camus, seems to require a greater degree of affirmation than he allowed himself in *L'Étranger*. But in his second novel, *La Peste*, he does present a more positive attitude to human destiny. This novel is one of modest hope and determined endeavour in a way that *L'Étranger* was not, and in it Camus uses clear and unmistakable symbolism. Indeed, the whole conception and construction of *La Peste* make it one of the most impressive novels of recent times to which the term *roman-mythe* may be applied.

La Peste is an account of the fight against an imaginary epidemic—the 'plague' referred to in the title—which supposedly afflicted Oran sometime in the 1940s. Camus describes a particular event (the plague) in a geographical location (North Africa), but he handles his subject in such a way that he extends its meaning beyond the particular to the universal. He conveys a general picture of man's position in the universe, faced by the problem of evil and the necessity of suffering. In a less total fashion Camus also includes a series of indirect references to the German Occupation of France and so adds a second level of symbolical meaning to the novel. *La Peste* is thus an ambitious attempt to combine in one whole a literal and two metaphorical interpretations. In this way it contains a network of symbols—situations, characters and physical objects which, while being themselves, also represent other things beyond themselves.

So far I have spoken of *La Peste* as a *roman-mythe*. I have done so because this term is commonly applied to it in France and because it helps to place Camus' novel in the general context of modern myth-making. Yet my own impression is that the expression *roman-mythe,* like the word *mythe* itself, is often loosely and vaguely used by the French. . . . Used in this way a *roman-mythe* will sometimes mean an allegorical novel, sometimes a symbolist novel, sometimes any novel which adds a metaphysical dimension to the temporal events it describes. Such vagueness is better avoided; indeed it seems clear that the full significance of *La Peste,* at any rate, will be better understood by describing it more precisely. To begin with, it is not, strictly speaking, an allegorical novel. In an allegorical novel . . . two levels of interpretation are continuously maintained throughout. But a reading of *La Peste* shows that its symbolism, though frequent, is of an intermittent kind. There are certainly many moments when its narrative calls for an added, metaphorical interpretation, but there are also stretches of narrative which, as far as I can see, are to be taken at a literal level only. At the other extreme of classification, *La Peste* is clearly something more than a directly realistic account of dramatic contemporary events to which metaphysical meanings are added. It is a different kind of novel from those of Malraux or Graham Greene. Camus is not writing as the witness of some contemporary happening, as a reporter on real situations in Europe or Africa or Mexico or the Far East. Instead he has deliberately created an imaginary situation, an epidemic in Oran. He has chosen a situation which is also a symbol. It allows him to give an impression of realism but it is also a neat prefigurement of his own desperate metaphysic. The plague provides him both with the closed universe of the absurd (the town of Oran cut off from contact with the outside world) and with the necessity for revolt (the efforts of Dr. Rieux and others to combat the plague and reduce its lethal effects). . . .

In the light of these distinctions I propose to call *La Peste* a symbolist novel. By this I mean a novel in which the relationship between two or more levels of meaning is not so continuously sustained as in the allegory, yet is more complete and organic than in what might be called politico-metaphysical fiction. And such a symbolist novel, it should be noted, enables Camus to get the best of two worlds. In the pure allegory the literal level of meaning is often weak because of the constant strain of allegorical significance. Thus a book like *Gulliver's Travels* is enjoyed at the literal level mainly by children, whereas adults largely ignore this aspect and treat seriously only its metaphorical meaning. In the politico-metaphysical novel, on the other hand, the emphasis is quite different. Here the 'realistic' element is most powerful. The particular human drama described is of prime interest to most readers and possible metaphysical interpretations come rather as an afterthought. A symbolist novel like *La Peste* lies midway between these two types and possesses the best qualities of each. The close integration of both literal and metaphorical levels means that both are readily recognized by the reader and each is enjoyed for its own sake. The immediate story is not overstrained by the need for continuous allegorical reference. The interpretation of the symbol by the reader is not an unbroken process. Transition from one level to another is only called for intermittently and the non-literal aspect is all the more persuasive because it emerges at intervals, and not all the time, from a firmly and continuously realistic narrative.

I have said that *La Peste* is a typical example of an outstanding general feature in recent literature and thought. It is also worth pointing out, however, that this novel fits naturally into Camus' own ideal of fiction. . . . Camus claims that the novel has tended, throughout its history, either towards increased naturalism or greater formalism. Particularity and abstraction are the two poles by which it has been alternately attracted at different periods. But the novel has only been great, he claims, when it has been more or less equally attracted by both poles at once. Too ready a movement in either single direction has led to aesthetic heresy and a misunderstanding of the true nature of fiction. Camus thus claims that novels should take a middle path between the particular and the universal; that they will receive dimensional fullness only from a proper combination of both. Novels should hold the concrete and the abstract in a natural and closely knit proportion and balance. One would have to say, I think, that the symbolist novel is not the only way of obtaining this result, but it is also clear that the very nature of the symbol makes it one of the most obvious and natural means to such an end. The successful symbolist novel will combine the concrete and the abstract in an organically inevitable relationship. They will be as inseparable, and yet as distinguishable, as the flower and its scent or the memento and its associations. In this way the symbolist novel achieves that reconciliation of the singular and the universal desired by Hegel and described by Camus as the essential activity of art.

The symbolist novel, as we find it in *La Peste,* is not only consistent with Camus' interpretation of art but seems to be encouraged by his attitude to history. . . . In *La Peste* Camus is attempting to diagnose the human dilemma and offer some remedy for it. Yet his view of the nature of this dilemma is that it lies outside the resources of history. There is no temporal remedy that will meet the case. For this reason he avoids writing a novel which would seem to present the problem in purely temporal terms and offer a purely temporal solution. Instead, by means of a central and pervasive symbol, he is concerned to place the problem outside time. This is where he thinks the problem really belongs, and in *La Peste* he moves beyond the wastage of time to the conservation of the symbol. The plague, because it must first assume concrete and historical form, enables *La Peste* to be a philosophical novel and not simply a philosophical treatise. But since the plague is also a symbol possessing non-literal and non-temporal meaning, it allows this same novel to discuss the problem of evil and of man's estrangement in the universe in those non-historical terms which Camus requires.

One final word should be said concerning the critical approach to *La Peste* before coming to examine it in more detail. This is a matter on which Camus has expressed himself indirectly in his essay on Kafka (added to the later editions of *Le Mythe de Sisyphe*). His opening remark is that Kafka puts the reader under an obligation to read him twice. The nature of the symbolist novel requires two readings—one for each of the two levels of interpretation which even the simplest symbol contains. But one should add, I think, that a third reading is also necessary. Having responded as completely as possible to the literal and latent meanings of the symbol, the critic should then read the novel again so as to reconstitute it in its organic duality. Only in this way, and at this third reading, can one fully appreciate the richness of texture and the continuous interplay of the explicit and the implicit which are a fundamental part of the symbolist novel's effect on the reader. The real justification for taking the symbol apart and distinguishing its literal and non-literal aspects is the increased response to its recreated wholeness which such a procedure makes possible. . . .

Camus indicates the symbolical nature of *La Peste* on the title-page. He takes his epigraph from Defoe's preface to the third volume of *Robinson Crusoe:* '. . . it is as reasonable to represent one kind of imprisonment by another, as it is to represent anything that really exists by that which exists not'. He goes farther than Defoe, however. As I have already pointed out, he derives *two* figurative meanings from the symbol of the plague since there are clear and repeated allusions both to the German Occupation and to man's metaphysical dereliction in the world. Camus appears to have conceived his theme and his symbol originally in 1939, and this obviously means that he first thought of it in terms of the plague/problem of evil analogy only. But the writing of *La Peste* in its final form did not begin until 1944. By this time Camus' experience of the Occupation had strongly suggested a further analogy which the original image of the plague seemed capable of absorbing. No doubt this further level of meaning was also prompted, if only verbally, by the common French description of Hitler's armies as *'la peste brune'.* At all events it is not surprising that by 1944 the Occupation aspect had become of considerable importance in the novel. In a letter to Roland Barthes, Camus himself has said that *La Peste* is, in a sense, more than a chronicle of the Resistance but that it is also certainly no less than this.

Here, then, we have a symbolist novel which, through historical chance, possesses two major figurative interpretations. Later I shall have to discuss how far the plague is a satisfactory symbol at each of these two levels, but for the moment I only wish to emphasize its potential richness and scope. Sartre has rightly spoken of the way in which the plague-symbol gives organic unity to a plurality of critical and constructive themes, but its richness can also be seen from a slightly different angle. In *La Peste* we have an image which expands to universal significance through three stages. It speaks directly of individual life and indirectly of politics and metaphysics. Thus the three major areas of human experience are included—the personal, the social, the speculative—and all three are unified in the symbol of the plague. In this way Camus attempts, through his novel, to make contact with the whole experience of man, with the triple living and thinking of the reader.

At the literal level *La Peste* has very little plot. The narrative, which is absorbing for all that, simply follows the natural curve of the plague from its beginnings, through its period of lethal intensity, to its eventual disappearance. The plague is first indicated by the large number of rats lying dead in the houses and streets of Oran. Soon, human beings also begin to die, stricken by inflammatory swellings in the groin and armpit. When the number of deaths rises steeply the Government admits the fact of the plague, Oran is shut off from the outside world, various measures are taken and serums tried. For months the plague rages unabated, however, and no effective answer can be found. Eventually one person recovers despite having had the dreaded symptoms, and others gradually follow. In time the illness becomes much less common, the death-rate falls sharply, and finally the plague disappears in as apparently arbitrary a fashion as it first arrived. During the period of the plague, which is described with something approaching scientific detachment and exactness, the reactions of the inhabitants are also reported. The attitudes of some individuals, but mainly of the population as a whole—fear or indifference or escapism—are described. Lastly, the fight against the plague, the different attempts to overcome it by medicine or heroism or prayer, is studied in the principal characters, who include Dr. Rieux, Tarrou, Rambert, Grand and Father Paneloux. It is Dr. Rieux who tells the story, though this does not become clear until near the end of the book.

As regards this literal level—the story purely as a 'realistic' account of an epidemic—it is significant that Camus chooses to call *La Peste* a *chronique,* not a *roman.* Whereas, in *L'Étranger,* he used the method of direct presentation, he chooses here the vehicle of detached narration. The situation is reported on objectively in *La Peste:* it is not subjectively embodied and recreated as in *L'Étranger.* This desire for objectivity is stated at various times in the novel. We read, for example:

> . . . in order to give nothing away, and especially not himself, the narrator has aimed at objectivity. His desire has been to change nothing by means of artistic devices, except where this has been necessary in the straightforward interests of a more or less coherent story.

This objective narration, the method of the chronicle, serves an important purpose in the symbolist novel. Although in a sense it reinforces the authenticity of events at the literal level, it also holds the reader at some distance from these events. The reader, conscious of the presence of the objective narrator, the chronicler, is prevented from identifying himself fully with the characters and their situation. This detachment from reality, which exists side by side with acceptance of it, makes the reader potentially more receptive to the further implications of the symbol. It enables him to transfer his attention more easily from the literal to the figurative level. At the same time it means that the 'realism' can be thoroughly indulged in without the symbolical inferences being weakened. This strengthening of the straightforward 'story' aspect clearly makes for a better symbolist novel and even adds to the power of the symbol itself. And the two most common snares of the symbolist novel, obvious didacticism or excessive abstraction, are most likely to be avoided by the objective narrative method of the chronicle.

One of the main difficulties of the symbolist novel, at the realistic level, lies in the presentation of the characters. Characters such as Rieux, Tarrou and Grand are by no means mere puppets voicing ideas, yet it remains true that we do not have a very clear picture of them. The chronicle method in *La Peste* holds us at a distance from them, and in general they do not have psychological density or completely convincing personalities. This point suggests two comments. Firstly, Camus only claims to have written a *chronique,* not a *roman.* He shows a careful discrimination in such matters reminiscent of Gide's distinctions, in his own work, between *roman, récit* and s*otie.* There is therefore some point in accepting *La Peste* for what it is. The presentation of character which it contains is entirely consistent with Camus' own classification of it as a literary form. To complain that the characters are psychologically flat and not sufficiently individualized is to ask for a different genre from that which Camus set out to give us. Secondly—and this is perhaps a more important point—all the major characters in *La Peste* do have strongly marked *moral* features. In their reactions to a sudden and overwhelming catastrophe, the plague, they are clearly defined and focused. They are presented to us in an extreme situation and it is with their behaviour in the face of this situation that Camus is concerned. Furthermore, the primary aim in *La Peste* is to portray a collective reaction to a collective problem. Private solutions of personal dilemmas are secondary—sometimes even irrelevant. And so Camus is concerned to give his main characters general moral features rather than individual psychological aspects. And this, one may add, is in keeping with his own statement, in which he echoes Malraux, that the emphasis in literature has shifted from psychology to metaphysics.

Before leaving these matters of narrative method and characterization in *La Peste* one further feature should be mentioned. Camus tells his story through a first-person narrator who maintains a strict anonymity until the final chapter. He then reveals himself as Dr. Rieux, the chief character in the book. The narrative method here is largely the reverse of that in *L'Étranger.* Meursault revealed himself directly to the reader in recounting events towards which he felt a complete outsider. His way of telling his story emphasized his rôle as a victim. Conversely, Rieux conceals his identity from the reader while speaking of events in which he is deeply involved. His way of telling his story emphasizes his rôle as a witness, and he is as deeply committed in act as he is detached in narration. In this way Camus may be said to present Rieux's personal story impersonally. He avoids abstraction and maintains 'human interest' by using Rieux as narrator, but he makes him narrate in a way that ultimately assists the universalizing intention of the symbol. This universalizing intention appears in Rieux's explanation of his lengthy and strict anonymity:

> When tempted to blend his own secret directly with the
> voices of a thousand plague victims he was stopped by the
> thought that each one of his sufferings was also experienced
> by the others and that this was an advantage in a world
> where suffering is so often solitary. Clearly he had to speak
> on behalf of everybody.

The narrative effect obtained by Camus in *La Peste* is thus
one which arouses the reader's interest by means of an individual who then directs it away from himself towards a
representative group of human beings. Rieux is used as the
narrator first to focus the reader's attention and then to diffuse it again. In this way Camus attempts to obtain that extension of interest beyond individual psychology to the general human condition which he holds to be a major feature
of contemporary writing of the highest quality.

I now turn to the first of the two figurative levels of *La
Peste*—the plague as a symbol of the Occupation. At this level
there are many obvious analogies to be made. Among a
large number of possible examples one may mention the
confusion of public opinion and the feeling of stupefaction
when the presence of the plague is finally accepted as a reality (p. 48); the rationing of food and petrol, the growing
electricity cuts and the disappearance of most of the town's
traffic (p. 94); the restrictive measures announced by the
press and the increased police surveillance (p. 130); the
growth of 'resistance' against the plague (p. 151); Cottard's
'black-market' activities (pp. 160–1); the mass burial of victims of the plague in open graves (p. 198); the isolation
camps with their loud-speakers (p. 267); the growing hopes
of liberation from the plague, the rejoicing at its disappearance, the later reprisals and the beating-up of Cottard (pp.
293, 298, 330–3).

The advantages of this symbolical treatment of the Occupation are no doubt obvious. . . . By rejecting a directly realistic account of the Occupation, Camus also removes his narrative from the sphere of personal passion and private bias.
Symbolic presentation enables him to avoid those contemporary pressures which have lessened the value of so many accounts of the Occupation and Liberation. The use of the symbol also enables him to increase the scope of his narrative so
as to include all political tyrannies. At the first figurative
level his symbol is an expanding one ranging outward in
space and backward in time. From an epidemic in Oran it extends to the German Occupation of France, then of Western

Europe, then to any dictatorship—Hitlerian or Stalinist—and finally it contains features common to the tyrannies of the past as well as of recent history. I think that a realization of this extension of the symbol lay behind some of the most intelligent, and most severe, criticism of *La Peste* by Marxists in France. And Camus seems to be referring to this fact when he says in the letter to Barthes mentioned above: 'No doubt this is why they reproach me—because *La Peste* can serve any resistance to any kind of tyranny'.

Criticisms of another kind, however, can and should be made against the Occupation aspect of *La Peste*. In a way, of course, the symbol of the plague is an ideal image of the Occupation, yet in several important respects its validity breaks down. For example, the moral dilemmas of the Occupation are almost entirely absent from this symbolical representation. The difficult debates about ends and means, or the difficult responsibility of choosing to kill a German soldier thereby causing, perhaps, the deaths of a dozen French hostages—these are aspects which the symbol fails to cover. Within the context of the plague, at least as Camus presents it, right actions are clear once one has chosen to struggle against it. But in the case of the Occupation acute problems of action arose precisely because one had chosen to resist. Another inadequacy is the weakness of the plague as a symbol of man's inhumanity to man. There is a disturbing moral ambiguity present in such products of human agency as war, oppression and injustice, but this ambiguity is entirely absent in *La Peste*. By using the plague as his symbol, and by emphasizing its arbitrary nature, Camus places political evil in a phenomenon existing outside the scope of human responsibility. It appears to me that at this point Camus falls victim of the extreme humanist fallacy of a perfect, or perfectible, human nature. He avoids facing the problem of the evil that results from human actions—presumably because this might lead him to a logical acceptance of some kind of deity. By using the symbol of the plague, however, he puts war and its attendant evils on a level with natural catastrophes such as earthquakes or avalanches—phenomena beyond the apparent responsibility of man. He equates war with the plague, evil with illness, and then looks round for humanist medicaments. One has to admit, of course, that this attitude to the Occupation is strictly in keeping with Camus' own metaphysical views. It is consistent with his sensitivity to human suffering and death, combined with his disbelief in God. For my own part, however, I am unable to avoid the conviction that Camus' symbol of the plague is inadequate at the Occupation level. I find it appropriate in the context of suffering but unsatisfactory before the fact of wrong-doing. It covers human wretchedness but ignores human wickedness. And so the whole picture of the Occupation in *La Peste* seems to me to have been morally simplified. There is never any question of the right things being done for the wrong reasons, of evil consequences following uncontrollably from virtuous motives, etc. The plague offers many circumstantial similarities to the Occupation, but it is powerless to convey a sense of its human agency and moral ambiguity.

Such features in this symbol, although they weaken its political interpretation, strengthen its metaphysical application. At this third level Camus is concerned with the problem of evil in the sense of suffering, not wrong-doing. For this purpose the plague is an admirable vehicle. It is arbitrary. Its appearance and disappearance are ultimately beyond the scope of human agency. It is terrible in its effects and little known in its origins. It is a familiar catastrophe, yet an apparently unavoidable one. Among the many features of the plague, however, its spatially concentrated and temporally undifferentiated character makes it a particularly suitable medium for the expression of Camus' metaphysical ideas. The town of Oran is sealed off on one side by the sea. On the other side, once the fact of the epidemic has been recognized and accepted, the gates are closed to prevent the spread of infection. This picture of Oran, isolated by geography and catastrophe, provides another version of that 'univers clos' which Camus finds in Lucretius, Sade, the Romantics, Nietzsche, Lautréamont, Rimbaud, the surrealists and various more recent writers. He discusses this question at the beginning of Part IV of *L'Homme révolté* and claims that metaphysical revolt has always found expression either in a special rhetoric or in the image of a closed universe. Within the limitation and concentration of the closed universe writers in metaphysical revolt have looked for the coherence and unity on which to base a new metaphysic. The plague thus has a spatially confined and unified setting whose very narrowness and concentration enable it to take on universal significance.

A similar effect is obtained by the temporal quality of the epidemic. For most of the duration of the plague time is experienced by the inhabitants of Oran as mere undifferentiated succession. Temporal relationships, or an interpretative historical pattern, are notably absent. The chronicle method of telling the story reinforces this impression of unmeasured time. There is movement and flow, but no explanation or evaluation. The result is a kind of ideal, abstract time which again strengthens the universal aspect of the symbol and makes its metaphysical application all the more natural and smooth.

La Peste, then, with its picture of the inhabitants of Oran cut off from the rest of the world and suffering and dying from the epidemic, is a picture of cosmic alienation, of that metaphysical absurdity of man's condition analysed in *Le Mythe de Sisyphe.* The feature of the absurd which is particularly emphasized in *La Peste,* and against which Camus revolts most strongly, is the problem of evil. As I have already suggested he uses the plague as a symbol of suffering, of that human wretchedness and pain which is a major aspect of the problem of evil. This is a subject which preoccupies Camus. There are repeated references to it in his writings. The following statement, made in the course of a talk given to the Dominicans of Latour-Maubourg in 1948, is a brief but typical formulation of his attitude: 'I share your horror of evil. But I do not share your optimism, and I continue to struggle against this universe in which children suffer and die.' The problem of evil, in this sense, is particularly concentrated round two sermons preached by the Jesuit Father Paneloux. The first sermon, recalling in several ways the fiery rhetoric of another Jesuit Father in *A Portrait of the Artist as a Young Man,* is preached during the early days of the plague. Father Paneloux interprets the plague as being divine in origin and punitive in purpose, a fitting judgment on the sins of Oran. He emphasizes his point that evil as a method of punishment is an instrument for good. . . .

Father Paneloux's second sermon on the plague is preached shortly after the death of Othon's son. It differs markedly from the earlier one in that he now speaks of 'we' rather than 'you'. There is much greater humility, and a certain hesitancy in his manner and phrasing. Although he still maintains that good finally comes out of evil he now says that this belief cannot be demonstrated rationally but must be accepted by faith. He goes on to distinguish—moved again by the death of Othon's child—between necessary suffering (e.g. Don Juan in Hell) and apparently unnecessary suffering (e.g. the child slowly and painfully killed by the plague). He also refuses as too facile the argument that earthly pain is compensated by eternal bliss. And so the problem of evil brings one to the cross-roads of complete faith or complete disbelief. Father Paneloux is not afraid to use the word 'fatalism' in connection with the attitude which he finally commends. But it must be an active fatalism which leaps into the heart of the unacceptable by an act of positive choice.

I have spent some time summarizing these two sermons, partly because they deal with a central theme in *La Peste*, but mainly to show how metaphysical—or theological—considerations can arise directly at the literal level. This latter feature also helps, I think, to make one accept more readily the broader metaphysical implications of the second figurative level. The direct metaphysics of the sermons prepares the reader's mind for the effort of grasping the indirect metaphysics of the novel as a whole. This is also further evidence of the close integration existing between the concrete and abstract aspects of the symbol. Many secondary symbols connected with the *univers clos* might also be mentioned—the sea, for example, or the window towards which Rieux turns at several crucial moments. But enough has perhaps been said to show what Camus' purpose is and how he sets out to achieve it. One should add, of course, that although the preceding analysis may have some purpose the symbol can only be finally judged as it comes through during a direct reading of the novel. During such a reading it operates either on all three levels at once, or by swift transitions from one to another. In this way the novel is provided with an admirable focus. The symbol of the plague combines everyday elements with political and metaphysical ones in a powerful and pervasive single image. Each level of presentation gains something by its simultaneous meaning at a different level. Not only do all the themes in the book issue from the dominant image of the plague; they meet in it again with renewed significance.

Camus Is a Positive Pessimist

Derek Parker

In the following viewpoint, Derek Parker interprets Camus's message as that of a positive pessimist. Parker asserts that Tarrou functions as a mouthpiece for Camus's own views, connecting the words of the character to the author's personal experiences. Parker analyzes *The Plague* as an allegory for the Nazi occupation and interprets the novel's broader meanings—"the notion of existence in general."

On this earth there are pestilences and there are victims, and it's up to us, so far as possible, not to join forces with the pestilences. That may sound simple to the point of childishness; I can't judge if it's simple, but I know it's true.

The words of Tarrou, a stranger who comes to the plague-stricken city of Oran and selflessly devotes himself to the struggle against the epidemic, might have been the words of Camus himself—of a born pessimist struggling unavailingly towards optimism, and in the end only reaching a compromise with despair.

Albert Camus was born in Mondovi, Algeria, on 7 November 1913. The son of an illiterate agricultural worker who, when the boy was eight months old, went off to the Great War and fell at the first battle of the Marne. Camus's mother, also illiterate, took him, his elder brother Lucien, and his grandmother off to Algiers, where she supported the family by working as a charwoman. Camus grew up in the streets, contending with dogs and other children for the contents of dustbins. His mother sent him to the local primary school, where a teacher, recognizing his quickness, gave him extra lessons and persuaded his mother to let him sit for a scholarship to the *lycée*, which he won. In 1957, Camus dedicated his speech accepting the Nobel Prize for Literature to that teacher, Louis Germain.

Reprinted from Derek Parker, "Introduction," in *The Plague*, written by Albert Camus. Introduction © 1987 The Folio Society, renewed © 2000 Derek Parker. Reprinted with permission from The Folio Society, Ltd., London.

His life at the *lycée* was that of any student: he worked
well, but much of his energy was devoted to sports—swim-
ming, but above all football: he was goal-keeper for a club
called the 'Racing Universitaire d'Alger', and used to claim
that he learned ethics on the football field. In his late teens,
he left home, sold car accessories, worked as a clerk, produced a report on barometric pressure in South Algeria for
the Institute of Meteorology and became the actor-manager
of a touring left-wing theatre group, before deciding to make
a living as a writer. His diploma paper for his *licence* was on
the influence of Plotinus on St Augustine—written while he
was a member of the Communist Party, which he joined in
1934, being instructed to teach Marxism to the Muslims. A
sudden reverse of policy made without warning, consultation
or excuse outraged him, and he resigned. But it may be that
Tarrou's 'confession' in *The Plague* sheds a further light on
Camus's attitude to the Party. Tarrou's concern was that the
social order around him was based on capital punishment:

> I was told that these few deaths were inevitable for the build-
> ing up of a new world in which murder would cease to be . . .
> I learned that I had had an indirect hand in the deaths of
> thousands of people; that I'd even brought about their deaths
> by approving of acts and principles which could only end that
> way . . . Even those who were better than the rest could not
> keep themselves nowadays from killing or letting others kill,
> because such is the logic by which they live; and that we can't
> stir a finger in this world without bringing death to some-
> body. Yes, I've been ashamed ever since; I have realised that
> we all have plague.

We can safely take Tarrou's view to be that of the author:
Camus's *Réflexions sur la Guillotine*, which appeared in the
Nouvelle Revue Française in 1957, remains one of the most
persuasive and cogent arguments against capital punishment ever to have been published. And it is Tarrou's profoundly pessimistic attitude, not only to the random universe but to man's behaviour in it, which is at the heart of
The Plague—La Peste—published in June, 1947, five years
after *The Outsider—L'Etranger*—which had made him famous overnight. When war broke out, Camus was editing a
left-wing newspaper in Algeria. It seems to have been the
news of the Nazi execution of the Communist leader Gabriel
Peri which persuaded him to go to France, and to work there
for the resistance until the liberation.

L'Etranger (which most critics claim as Camus's masterpiece) came out in 1942. It is the story of a man who has lived a simple life devoted to pleasure, kills an Arab (perhaps in self-defence) and is executed after an incompetent trial. It is indeed a remarkable book, but the timing of its publication contributed to its initial success. *Le Mythe de Sisyphe*, which followed it a few months later, asserted that life was meaningless; in the circumstances of the time that too struck a chord. Then came two plays, *Le Malentendu* and *Caligula*, and then *La Peste*, which sold a hundred thousand copies within a few months.

AN ALLEGORY FOR THE OCCUPATION

The Plague is virtually plotless—like Defoe's *Journal of the Plague Year*. It simply tells of the reactions of a group of men to the horrors of pestilence. Yet not, after all, so simply. *The Plague* has, in the first place, been seen as a book 'about' France under Nazi occupation. And indeed Camus asserted, 'I wish to express through the plague the suffocation which we have all suffered, and the atmosphere of threat and exile in which we have lived'; while in 1955 he told Roland Barthes that he explicitly wanted to show the nature of the French resistance against the Nazis.

The parallels are obvious. There are physical ones: the curfew; the shortage of electricity and food; the quarantine camp, so well-run ('We're great believers in efficiency in this camp!'). But the psychological pressures of isolation are paralleled, too—the suspicion that the outside world, while making gestures of sympathy, was really relatively impassive:

> Sometimes at midnight, in the great silence of the sleepbound town, the doctor turned on his wireless before going to bed for the few hours' sleep he allowed himself. And from the ends of the earth, across thousands of miles of land and sea, kindly, well-meaning speakers tried to voice their fellow-feeling, and indeed did so, but at the same time proved the utter incapacity of every man truly to share in suffering which he cannot see . . . 'Oran, we're with you!' they called emotionally. But not, the doctor told himself, to love or die together—and that's the only way.

It is a passage which rings true not only of France in 1942 but of Hungary in 1956, or Poland more recently. Cottard, the black-marketeer, and his reaction to the plague, recall the spirit of collaboration ('The plague suits me quite well, and I see no reason why I should bother about trying to stop it'), and the continual battle to hold on to some aspects of normality must be accurate enough: 'the long, heart-rending monotonous struggle put up by some obstinate people . . . to recover their lost happiness, and to balk the plague of that part of themselves which they were ready to defend in the last ditch.'

A BROADER CANVAS

But the novel is concerned with a broader canvas than that of France—or any other country—under a tyranny. 'I wanted to extend this interpretation to the notion of existence in general,' Camus said; and he is much concerned to examine the religious instinct in man, and how it stands up to the pressure of a dreadful reality 'under the vast indifference of the sky.'

Camus was an agnostic rather than an atheist, and his re-action to Christianity was resigned rather than antagonistic: 'the Christian world, with its faith, seems to me to be a de-spairing one,' he wrote, and in *The Plague* he illustrates this by contrasting the attitudes of Rieux, the doctor, and Pan-eloux, the priest. Paneloux, after witnessing the terrible death of a child, can only preach 'active resignation'; Rieux is not impressed by this—and Camus has prepared the ground by reporting Paneloux's first sermon, which the priest begins by telling his congregation: 'Calamity has come on you, my brethren, and, my brethren, you deserved it.'

The priest goes on to suggest that the time his flock had set aside for church-going and prayer had been insufficient:

These brief encounters [with God] could not sate the fierce hunger of His love. He wished to see you longer and more of-ten; that is His manner of loving and, indeed, it is the only manner of loving. And this is why, wearied of waiting for you to come to Him, He loosed on you this visitation; as He has visited all the cities that offended against Him, since the dawn of history.

This is not an unusual reaction by the Church under the pressure of calamitous events: one has to look no further than America to find a similar response from fundamentalist Christians to the scourge of AIDS: or, in this country, more farcical but no less remarkable, there was in 1984 the serious suggestion, in letters to *The Times,* that York Minster was set on fire by God as a judgement on the Church for admitting the Right Revd David Jenkins to the bishopric of Durham.

As a comment on the trials of the French people during

the Occupation the novel is less than fully convincing. As many critics have pointed out, plague is, after all, a natural disaster; it is, as Camus says elsewhere, 'external and un-avoidable'; it may provoke human cruelty and injustice, but the bacillus is not in itself 'responsible' for its evil conse-quences in the way in which man is responsible for the hor-ror and cruelty inflicted by the excesses of right- or left-wing regimes. Men have not to be killed by men in order to stop the spread of a plague.

It is Camus's view of man's response to an anarchic uni-verse which seems in the end most to interest himself, and about which he is most interesting. He concentrates to a large extent on Christianity not because he is himself anti-Christian, but because he is amazed that so many people continue to find that faith a satisfactory clue to the solution of the problem of the meaning of life. Scornful of this, what he hates is what he sees as the pessimism of the faith: the fact that Christians recognise injustice in the world, but condone it by accepting it as 'God's will'. So, he argues, to accept Chris-tianity is to accept evil, suffering, the death of innocents as part of a Divine Plan; he is not prepared to honour a God who is either powerless to prevent this, and therefore not worthy of worship, or all-powerful, and therefore guilty of evil.

A PLOTLESS NOVEL

That a plotless novel on such a theme should have had such a popular success, and should still be in demand forty years after its first publication, is a tribute not only to the univer-sal nature of the philosophical argument but, of course, also to the quality of the writing. *The Plague* is a beautifully con-structed novel in which the simplicity and immediacy of the style subtly change with the nature of each section. There is an uncanny stillness at the centre of the book, where despair seems to triumph; a growing liveliness as hope returns, and a strange dark weight towards the end, with Tarrou's death and Rieux's tragic news, reminding us yet again that 'Man was born unto trouble, as the sparks fly upwards'.

Among the devices is a remarkable use, in the back-ground, of the changing weather. Marvellous summer heat becomes malignant: 'the sun of the plague had killed all colours and sent all joy into exile.' As the pestilence rages, 'A smell of brine and seaweed came from the unseen and storm-tossed sea. And the city, emptied of all its inhabitants, palled in dust and loud with the shrilling of the wind, groaned like a lost island of the damned.' The 'fierce breath' of the plague beats on the body of a child with 'reiterated gusts' of fever before 'the storm-wind passed'; and as the wind beats the rain against the window of Tarrou's room, 'the storm lashing his body' shakes it as though it is 'buffeted by all the ravaging winds of heaven'.

Such devices *are* only devices; but they are used in a masterly fashion, and if *La Peste* is perhaps in its entirety less successful than *L'Etranger*, it is the more readable and better-constructed book.

A POSITIVE PESSIMIST

After the war, Camus worked in Paris as an editor with the publishing house of Gallimard. On 5 January 1960 he was killed in a car crash. He had said, the previous year, that his career was only just beginning. His personal creed was as irrational and resistant to proof as Christianity—he believed in the goodness of man, illustrated in *The Plague* by the way in which Rieux, Tarrou, Rambert, even the insignificant and rather comic civil servant Grand, work together against the pestilence. His compassion is not for a God tormented by the neglect of man, but for man alone in his suffering.

Camus was by no means a gloomy, introverted pessimist, but—if it is possible—a very positive one. His personal life was never securely happy: his first marriage lasted only a year; he was separated from his second wife by the war, and this isolation cut deeply (it is reflected in the inconsolable loneliness of the characters in *The Plague;* Rieux separated from his wife, Rambert, the journalist, from his mistress). But he was capable of great happiness—perhaps the best essay in *L'Envers et l'Endroit* (1937) is entitled *L'Amour de vivre*—and like Meursault, the condemned hero of *L'Etranger*, Camus was vividly aware how much he loved living, despite the ridiculous, farcical, meaningless nature of life. He believed in 'the noble claim of happiness' and the sanctity of friendship: he shared the famous view that E.M. Forster expressed in *What I Believe:* 'If I had to choose between betraying my country and betraying my friend, I hope I should have the guts to betray my country.' But at his back was always the rumble of time's winged chariot; 'there is no love of living without despair of life,' he wrote, and in a sense he is to be judged by the quality of that despair.

Despair, however, is no answer to the approaching totality of death. There was no answer, indeed, for Camus; and only one possible consolation. He once said that if he had to write a book on ethics, it would have one hundred pages, ninety-nine of which would be blank. On the last page would be written, 'I know only one duty, and that is to love'—even if that love is unacknowledged, perhaps even unexpressed, as was Rieux's love for his mother: 'One day she—or he—would die, without ever, all their lives long . . . making their affection known.'

It is another tragedy, and with no more, no less 'meaning' than the plague. And that? Towards the end of the book, as the city is rejoicing that the pestilence has finally withdrawn, Rieux goes to see an old patient of his, suffering from nothing more serious than asthma. The old man is scornful of the whole episode in Oran's history:

> 'All those folks were saying, "It was plague. We've had the plague here." You'd almost think they expected to be given medals for it. But what does that mean—"plague"? Just life, no more than that.'

Public and Private Spheres: Dilemmas in *The Plague*

David R. Ellison

David R. Ellison, the chairman of foreign languages and literatures at the University of Miami, examines *The Plague* in context with the other works of Camus. Ellison discusses the manner in which Camus reconciles the balance of the happiness of the individual—a theme explored in his earlier work—with the importance of the common good and collective action. This balancing act between the public and private spheres produces moral conflicts within the main characters, and their attempts to resolve these dilemmas provide the basis for interpreting the novel. Camus develops the themes of individual happiness, religious faith, abstraction, revolt and social action, exile and community through his characters, including Rieux's narration of the novel itself. Ellison also points out that to see *The Plague* simply as an allegorical representation of World War II is to ignore additional levels of meaning.

Like *Caligula*, *The Plague* can be read as the representation of absolute evil and of the efforts made by certain individuals to struggle against its power. Whereas in *Caligula* only Cherea and Scipio had the courage to face the tyrant and to force him (if only briefly) to consider the magnitude of his misdeeds, in *The Plague* a group of people band together and learn the value of common action. What separates Camus's novel from his play is the new emphasis placed on the theme of community or solidarity. Like the Enlightenment philosopher Jean-Jacques Rousseau, who theorized in *The Social Contract* that the welfare of the public at large was not the magnified mirror-image of each individual's happiness, but rather the product of the sacrifices and renunciations every person must make toward the difficult achievement of a common good, Albert Camus realized that the fight to contain and neutralize the plagues that have overcome twentieth-century civilization necessitates the surrender of egocentric goals and self-satisfied tranquillity. At the same time, however, Camus recognized and respected the inevitability of each human being's desire for personal happiness. The key interpretive issues of *The Plague* center in the delicate balancing of the personal and the public spheres; each of the novel's main characters attempts to find his own solution to the moral dilemmas that emerge from the conflict of these separate but equally compelling realms.

ABSTRACTION AND THE HAPPINESS OF THE INDIVIDUAL

During the first stages of the epidemic, the populace of Oran does not wish to recognize the reality of its new predicament. As increasingly large numbers of rats die in the streets and as more and more of the city's citizens fill the hospitals, it should be evident to everyone that "normal life" is no longer possible. Those who resist this realization cling to a desire for security and initially refuse to grasp the fundamental necessity for solidarity in the face of the all-encompassing crisis. This is the case for the journalist Rambert, who, on temporary assignment from Paris, declares to Rieux: "But I am not from here!" (*P 89*). To say that he is not *from* Oran means that the events *in* Oran do not concern him. In the important conversation between Rambert and Rieux that ensues, the former holds on desperately and blindly to his need for personal happiness, while anticipating, despite himself, the need for common action against the ravages of the plague. In attempting to counter the impeccable but unpleasant logic of the protagonist, Rambert asserts: "I know you are about to speak of public service. But the common good is composed of the happiness of each person" (*P 90*). As the novel progresses, Rambert learns that there is happiness, or at least fulfillment, in public service, and that a merely private happiness based on pleasure and contentment cannot be justified under the particular conditions created by the plague. In this sense, Rambert's political/social stance evolves from opposition to Rousseau's theories to an acceptance of their premises.

In the early period of his resistance to the reality of the epidemic, Rambert accuses Rieux of living "in abstraction"

(*P 91*). That is: the journalist implies that the essentially un-
fathomable disease with its mysterious origins is more important to the doctor than human happiness in its concrete-
ness. Rieux's response to Rambert does not occur audibly in
the conversation, but is available to the reader in the narrator's transcription of his inner reflections: "Yes, there was in
misfortune no small part of abstraction and unreality. But
when the abstraction begins to kill you, it becomes necessary to trouble yourself with the abstraction" (*P Ibid.*). At the
end of the passage, Rieux's conclusion on this issue fore-
shadows the primacy of common or group action that will
characterize the novel as a whole. The doctor, aided by his
diverse associates, will continue "the monotonous struggle
between the happiness of each person and the abstractions
of the plague, which constituted the entire life of our city
during this long period" (*P 94*).

In the specific context of Camus's second novel and its
central allegorical significance, the "abstraction" to which
the narrator refers is doubtless that of war (and war, in 1947,
meant World War II). Yet Camus uses this term elsewhere in
his nonfictional and directly political writings, in order to
express the unenviable position of humankind in the post-
war age of ideological struggle and nuclear armament. In
one of his most important essays on the perilous situation of
the immediate post-war era written in 1948 and entitled "Ni
Victimes Ni Bourreaux" ("Neither Victims Nor Execution-
ers"), Camus declares that we live in a world of "terror" in
which persuasion, rational discussion, and dialogue in general are no longer possible. He explains in these terms:

> we live in a world of abstraction, that of offices and machines,
> of absolute ideas and of Messianism without subtlety. We suf-
> focate among people who think they have a monopoly on truth,
> whether through their machines or ideas. And for all those
> who can live only in dialogue and in friendship with their fel-
> low humans, this silence is the end of the world (*V 119*).

. . . In Camus's eyes, the end of World War II brought with
it more problems than its conclusion had apparently solved.
Most importantly, the realm of "abstraction" could no longer
be limited to *one* specific plague against which people could
struggle with some degree of common purpose. The post-
war world, divided into ideological camps and seemingly on
the brink of a nuclear holocaust, had outstripped the capacity of individuals to comprehend its complexities. The tech-

nological age that was about to begin was not congenial to
Camus's Mediterranean philosophy, as we shall see in the
next chapter. For the moment, it is necessary to see in the
notion of "abstraction" not only a central (perhaps *the* central) issue in *The Plague*, but also a concept that will inform
Camus's political thought continually—in fact, until the end
of his life.

PANELOUX'S SERMONS AND THE PROBLEM OF RELIGION

For those citizens of Oran who believed in a Christian God,
the period of the plague was a particularly difficult ordeal.
The atheist found in the epidemic the manifestation of some
blind and malevolent force of nature that remained necessarily incomprehensible; the Christian, on the other hand,
was tempted to see in its outbreak the clear sign of God's
wrath. The "abstraction," in the mind of the believer, contained a message from on high that demanded his careful
deciphering. The individual to whom the task of interpreting
the divine signs fell was Paneloux, the intellectual and activist Jesuit priest.

In his first sermon (*Part Two, 95–102*), Paneloux evokes
past historical occurrences of the disease, beginning with
the plague visited upon Egypt by Jehovah that cleared the
way for the Exodus of the Israelites under the leadership of
Moses. Paneloux's point is that each time the plague returns,
it is to humble nonbelievers and warn believers against the
loosening of their faith. He begins his discourse with the
portentous words: "Brethren, you are living in misfortune,
brethren, you deserve your lot" (*P 97*). His purpose is to
demonstrate that what seems incomprehensible to the human mind originates in the grand design of God. Furthermore, according to the priest, it is precisely *within* the de-
structiveness of the pestilence that the believing Christian
can find "an exquisite ray of eternity" (*P 101*) that leads toward deliverance:

> this ray . . . manifests the will of God, which without fail
> transforms evil into good. Even today, through this progres-
> sion of death, anguish, and lamentation, it guides us toward
> essential silence and toward the principle of all life. There,
> my brethren, is the immense consolation I wanted to bring
> you so that you might not only take away with you chastizing
> words, but also a message of conciliation (*P Ibid.*).

Readers of *The Myth of Sisyphus* will recognize here the
logic of consolation that Camus had condemned in the Chris-

tian existentialists Chestov and Kierkegaard, the "metaphysical reversal" that transforms the fundamental absurdity of the human condition into a transcendentally grounded meaningfulness. At this early stage in the progression of the epidemic, Paneloux is able to appeal rather successfully to the conscience of his parishioners, and his sermon has a strong, bracing effect on the faith of his flock. When he delivers his second sermon, however (*Part Four, 219–27*), conditions have changed, and his further use of the same logic pushed to the extreme limit of its harshness falls largely on deaf ears. Between the time of the first sermon and the second, Paneloux, like all citizens of Oran, has lived surrounded by death; in particular, he has witnessed the agonizing death of Othon's young son. While standing at the child's bedside, he had to face the anger of Dr. Rieux, who had exclaimed, in an accusatory tone: "Now this child, at least, was innocent, you can't deny that!" (*P 216*). Paneloux's response—"But perhaps we must love what we cannot comprehend" (*P 217*)—provokes what is no doubt the most passionate outburst by Rieux in the novel: "No, my father . . . I have a different idea of love. And I will refuse to the death to love this creation in which children are tortured" (*P Ibid.*). In this instance, Rieux is uttering Camus's own personal opinion as a non-believing humanist, as the anti-existentialist theoretician of the absurd.

Paneloux shows courage in his second sermon in that he takes on directly the problem (or "scandal") of the death of innocent children and makes it his theme. It is as if he is speaking from the pulpit to Rieux, as if all his theological training and erudition are compressed into one argument in an implicit dialogue with his atheistic adversary. Once again, the logic is that of the "metaphysical reversal," but in this case the tone is more dramatic, more suffused with pathos. At the heart of his argument is an appeal to an all-or-nothing alternative: either one is a Christian or one is not; either one believes everything or nothing; if one's position vis-à-vis God is that of humility, such humility must be absolute; absolute faith and absolute humility presuppose that one accepts every manifestation of divine will, including the plague—otherwise one accepts nothing. Thus, in Paneloux's words (which are a very faithful echo of the Kierkegaardian "leap of faith"), as indirectly retranscribed by Rieux:

> it was necessary to leap into the very heart of this inacceptable alternative that was offered us, precisely so that we

might make our choice. The suffering of children was our bitter bread, but without this bread, our soul would perish of spiritual hunger (*P 224–25*).

Shortly after delivering his second sermon, Paneloux dies. He refuses all medical help and suffers in stoic silence. The man who has offered spiritual consolation to his parishioners does not accept the consolations of human science; his death is consequent, it follows the logic of his beliefs and actions. In the symmetrical juxtaposition of the two sermons at two radically different moments of the plague and in the confrontation between Rieux and Paneloux, Camus has granted a central position to religion in his novel. Although the author, like his narrator-protagonist, and in diametrical opposition to his foil Paneloux, refuses all forms of metaphysical consolation, he expresses clear admiration for a man who establishes his life on a strong moral foundation and who can live with the consequences of his choices. Like the classical playwright Corneille, who fills his tragedies with enemies who, in the end, can only have esteem for each other, Camus has created, in the Rieux-Paneloux dialogue, two antagonists who inescapably recognize each other's worth.

TARROU AND THE "HOUR OF FRIENDSHIP"

Toward the end of Part Four, at the very height of the novel's action, Camus inserts a scene between Dr. Rieux and Tarrou that constitutes both a crucial development on the multiple symbolic meanings of the plague and a welcome pause in the dramatic tension. Tarrou, Rieux and their associates have witnessed the suffering and death of innumerable individuals, and have reached the stage at which they are very nearly numb to the devastation of their environment. It is at this point that the two men enjoy what Tarrou calls an "hour of friendship"—an evening spent together away from the burdens of the day and their common service to the community (*P 244–55*).

Until this scene, Tarrou's past has been an enigma. The reader knows of him only through the shrewd and original observations of his diaries and through his faithful work in the Sanitary organization that he created. For the first time, as the novel reaches its crisis and dénouement, we hear Tarrou speak directly and unequivocally about his formative years. What he says is in the mode of a highly personal confession; yet what he reveals about himself has major implications for the overall meaning of *The Plague* as an aesthetic whole. We learn that Tarrou's father was a respected lawyer who, when he was not prosecuting criminals, enjoyed consulting railway timetables in his spare time. Significantly, he rarely traveled: what interested him were the multiple possible connections among places in the abstract, not the concrete experience of these places in their everyday reality. This fundamental trait of character—the love of abstraction—carried over into his professional life, as the young Tarrou was to discover. One day, in an effort to impress his son and interest him in the future pursuit of law, the prosecutor invited him to the courtroom. There, in a dazzling display of legal logic and rhetorical brilliance, Tarrou's father successfully obtained the death penalty for a man whom Tarrou merely remembered in his physical insignificance, as a "sandy-haired owl" (*P 248*). Most impressive to the son was the father's use of the term "the accused" to designate the man he was condemning to death; by using this expression, the prosecutor effectively eliminated the individuality and humanity of the man on trial.

For Tarrou, the remembrance of this one childhood scene was to remain at the center of his later political and social consciousness. In essence, all of his adult life was to be a revolt against his father's arrogant use of abstraction; and this abstraction derived from the latter's sure knowledge of his own innocence, in contradistinction to the clear guilt of "the accused." What Tarrou learned from his day in court is that no one human can presume to be innocent, that no person can arrogate the power to condemn another to die on the basis of a supposed ethical superiority. From this initial discovery, Tarrou concludes, first: "none of us could make the slightest gesture in this world without the risk of causing death" (*P 250–51*). Second, expressed in metaphorical terms, this meant that none of us could pretend to be healthy in a moral sense: we were all, in Tarrou's language, *des pestiférés*—carriers of the plague.

Unlike the majority of the inhabitants of Oran, for whom the plague represented an unjust intrusion from some mysterious "outside" or "beyond," a calamitous descent of evil into a luminous world, Tarrou knew, before ever reaching Oran, that all of us carry the plague within us, as a fundamental constitutive part of our being. Hence his only apparently paradoxical assertion: "What is natural is the microbe.

All the rest—health, integrity, purity, if you will—is the effect of the will, of a will that must never cease to be active"
(*P 251*). Tarrou's metaphorical use of the word "plague" to
signify the evil within each of us, our subservience to the seductions of "abstraction" in its various guises (including that
abstraction in reasoning that justifies the death penalty),
adds a level of connotative potential to the allegory of the
novel. To reduce *The Plague* to a mere literary transposition
of World War II is to overlook the pertinence of Tarrou's reflections: indeed, if the plague that descends on Oran "is" the
War, it is only too easy to reduce the entirety of Camus's fiction to a simple mechanical allegory of Good (Rieux, Tarrou,
the Sanitary team as Resistance fighters) versus Evil (the
epidemic as objective correlative of Hitler's holocaust). But if
we take Tarrou's observations seriously, we discover a more
sobering message: namely, that the inherent tendency toward evil that exists in each human being must be coun-
tered daily by an act of the will. Innocence being impossible
and, in the strictest sense, irretrievable, the attempt to live
morally (i.e., our effort *not* to carry the plague) becomes a
properly Sisyphian task. Camus has progressed a great distance from the Romantic pathos of *The Stranger*, in which
Meursault could proclaim his essential innocence until the
moment of his "unjustified" execution. In *The Plague*, although Tarrou has killed no Arab on a beach, he knows that
his every action contains the potential for death. The world
of *The Stranger* was that of an individual pursuing his existence in a solitary daydream state; the world of *The Plague* is
that of a community in which each individual must adopt an
active wakefulness so as not to lapse into the tempting habits
of the prosecutor standing in judgment over his neighbor.

At the end of the scene, to seal their friendship, Rieux and
Tarrou take a nocturnal swim in the ocean. In this one exceptional moment of respite, human solidarity becomes a
reality. The silent communication that acts as a bond between the two men also serves as a poetic counterbalance to
the stark philosophy Tarrou had expounded earlier in the
chapter: by merely being together *as* friends enveloped in
the natural force of the tides, Rieux and Tarrou incorporate
the promise of deliverance from the abstractions of the
plague. As they swim together, side by side in the same
rhythm, their conjugated movements illustrate the possibility of overcoming the "permanent exile" (*P 252*) to which

Tarrou said he had condemned himself. This promise or possibility emerges in the only lyrical moment of the novel, and that moment is short-lived. Yet its very fragility haunts the remainder of Rieux's chronicle and stands as a reminder of the hope that never quite disappears from a city permeated with death.

NARRATION: THE ART OF BEARING WITNESS

From a technical standpoint, the most unusual feature of *The Plague* is its masking, until the final chapter of Part Five, of the narrator's identity. It is only in the concluding pages of the novel that Dr. Rieux steps forward to assume responsibility for the account we have just read and to justify his procedure. On the simplest level, the choice of Rieux as narrator is logical in that he is in a position, as medical doctor, to observe the ravages of the plague first-hand. Further, as a member of the Sanitary brigades organized by Tarrou, he is able to describe his fellow-citizens from close range. And finally, in his struggle with separation and exile (his wife, being away from Oran in a clinic, can offer him no support, and he is deprived of news on her condition), he shares the suffering of those whom he helps on a daily basis. Rieux explains (*P 302–03*) that he has tried to be as objective as possible: he has attempted not to "mix in a direct way his own personal impressions with the thousand voices of those afflicted with the plague." Thus, his method of narration can most properly be described as a *témoignage*, or bearing witness. In *The Plague*, we are far removed from the personal tone of *The Stranger* or from the confessional hyperbole of *The Fall*. To bear witness is to efface oneself in order to better express the physical and spiritual state of an entire community. And in so doing, in Rieux's own words, "he wished to be reunited with his fellow-citizens in the only certainties they had in common, which are love, suffering, and exile." Paradoxically, therefore, it is through a sober, neutral style that does not call attention to itself that Rieux is best able to reach the emotional depths within which the people of Oran were forced to descend during the period of the plague.

At the moment of deliverance from the epidemic, which Rieux describes in terms that must have brought to mind the Liberation of Paris to many Frenchmen in 1947, the desire for personal happiness reasserts itself powerfully, as couples and families are united once again. In evoking one last time

the essential differences between the sacrifice of self that
characterized the era of the plague and the yearning for
pleasure that had been dormant but always present in all individuals, the narrator opposes the crucial terms *exil* (exile)
and *patrie* (homeland). With forced imprisonment or exile
now a thing of the past, the citizens of Oran begin to think of
their *patrie,* which can be found "beyond the walls of this
suffocated city. It [*la patrie*] was in these sweet-smelling
thickets on the hillsides, in the ocean, the free land and the
weight of love" (*P 299*). This opposition—between exile and
a certain homeland or "kingdom"—will inform the last series of short stories written by Camus in 1957. In *The Plague,*
the novelist chose to depict a situation in which the promise
of a return to one's personal homeland is kept in near-
constant abeyance by the stifling omnipresence of an epidemic signifying the absolute of human evil. Through Dr.
Rieux's narrative conscientiousness, through his refusal to
do more than bear witness, we as readers can never suc-
cumb to the premature hope of an escape from exile. Yet in
his later works—in the essays and fictions of the 1950s—Camus returns to the problem of the relative place (or value) of
his two oppositional terms, in an attempt to justify philosophically and ground ethically the urge for a homeland that
inhabits us all, and that disappears only briefly, when we
fall prey to the catastrophes of our own making. At the very
end of his narrative commentary, Dr. Rieux suggests that although Tarrou's refusal of all consolations, his willingness
to live in a world completely devoid of hope, could be considered admirable, nevertheless for the majority of people
such an attitude is impossible. In Rieux's consciousness
there is room not only for the events of the present in their
current horror, but also for a world of sea and sky that can
never be erased as long as human beings have the courage
to refuse the enslavement brought on by the plagues of
which they are, unfortunately, the carriers.

The Plague as an Exploration of the Absurd

Brian Masters

Brian Masters, a scholar who frequently contributes to Great Britain's prestigious magazine, *The Spectator*, contemplates Camus's use of the theme of the Absurd in *The Plague* (referred to as *La Peste* by Masters). The Absurd is the absence of reason under which humanity must suffer, an awareness of life's misery in the search for significance in a world without meaning. Masters explains that Camus defines the Absurd in his earlier work, *The Myth of Sisyphus (Le Mythe de Sisyphe),* and later incorporates it fictitiously as a major theme in *The Plague,* with a new emphasis on collective opposition against this aspect of the human condition. Masters demonstrates how Camus develops the awareness of the Absurd through the setting of Oran, as well as the inappropriate responses to the Absurd by Cottard—who attempts suicide, despairs, and finally acquiesces to the plague—and Father Paneloux, who is guilty of the resignation of metaphysical hope. Also, Masters suggests that Camus's belief in the innate goodness of humanity and his prescription for collective struggle against adversity mark the writer as a humanist. Masters concludes by interpreting the symbolism of the plague, which he believes is an incarnation of the Absurd.

Of the possible responses to a discovery of the part played by the Absurd in human endeavour, enumerated by Camus in *Le Mythe de Sisyphe,* some have already found fictional illustration. Martha in *Le Malentendu* capitulated to the Absurd by committing suicide, Caligula in the play of that

name allied himself with the Absurd against mankind by in-
tensifying its power. In *La Peste* the only response worthy of
man, the position of revolt, is given eloquent expression. It
shows how it is possible to acknowledge the fact of the Absurd, without evasion or illusion, and yet not surrender to it.
La Peste also embodies an altruism absent from earlier
works and barely suggested by Cherea in *Caligula*. While
L'Etranger showed the individual moment of awareness,
and *Le Mythe de Sisyphe* an individual opposition against the
Absurd, *La Peste* is a portrait of collective struggle. Camus
has emerged from his introspective phase, a fact which he
recognized himself in a letter to Roland Barthes:

> *Pléiade*, p. 1966. 'Compared to *L'Etranger*, *La Peste* does rep-
> resent, beyond any possible discussion, the movement from
> an attitude of solitary revolt to the recognition of a commu-
> nity whose struggles must be shared.'

La Peste is one of those rare books which are so rich that
they can withstand interpretation on a dozen different levels
without suffering diminishment. It is a thoroughly gripping
novel, an allegory with many tentacles, and a personal statement of belief. The plague itself can represent whatever the
reader finds most objectionable or unendurable in human
life, and is thus subject to an infinite variety of symbolic interpretations. However, one symbol can contain them all, I
think, and that is the plague as a personification of the Absurd, remembering that the Absurd is Camus's shorthand
word to describe the lack of reason in the human condition.
This will do to start with, at least, though the image will become denser as we proceed.

There is virtually no plot. Camus describes the reactions
of half a dozen characters to the advent of a plague, inviting
the reader (even guiding him) to draw certain conclusions
from these reactions. The relationship of the characters with
each other is not examined. Camus is less interested in what
people say and do to each other than in what they say and do
about their ultimate destiny. He admitted as much when he
wrote, in *L'Envers et L'Endroit*, p. 25. 'I have learnt less about
people, since I am interested more in their destiny than in
their reactions.' This gives rise to a certain impersonality in
the narrative, so that the reader has the impression that he
is being preached at, that Camus is getting him by the shoul-
ders, giving him a vigorous shake, and telling him to listen.

The work is described by Camus as a 'chronique', a word

which implies objectivity and detachment. It is constructed
with the care, shape, and beauty of a classical symphony
(Mozart was Camus's great love). There are five parts, rising
in length and tension until the third part, when the plague is
at its apogée, and then *diminuendo* until it finally disappears. The scene is Oran, a town in Algeria, an ordinary
place like anywhere else, says Camus. . . . The narrator, Dr
Rieux, stumbles over a dead rat in the first sentence of the
second chapter of Part I. More dead rats appear, as Camus
introduces us one by one to his characters, and mysterious
illnesses suggest an epidemic. Dr Rieux is the first to recognize the truth, that they have a plague on their hands, but the
authorities are slow to agree. Eventually, the truth is so obvious that no one can deny it, and Camus concentrates on
the attitudes towards the truth exemplified by Rieux, Tarrou,
Rambert, Paneloux, Grand and Cottard. The struggle is long
and arduous, Rambert and Cottard are profoundly changed
as a result, Tarrou and Paneloux both die of the plague, Cottard is killed by the police. When the plague has receded, the
gates of Oran are opened again, but the reader is left with an
uneasy feeling that this is not the end of the matter, that the
events related might occur again, somewhere else, and that
they might concern him.

Camus creates this impression by insisting on the banality and ordinariness of life in Oran. 'Really, all that was to be
conveyed was the banality of the town's appearance and of
life in it.' The people of Oran (like the people in *L'Etranger)*
are dominated by habits which have erected a screen between themselves and their awareness of life. Their existence follows a stagnant pattern, best illustrated by the little
old man who amuses himself by spitting on cats from his
window and who does not know what to do with himself
when the plague robs him of cats (p. 130), and by the asthmatic whose day is ruled by the counting of peas. He has two
saucepans; he transfers peas, one by one, from one saucepan
to the other. When the exercise has been completed, he
knows it is time he had something to eat (p. 133). Camus has
got to create an atmosphere of boredom both to remind us
that there is nothing special about Oran, and what happened
there could be relevant to us, and to prepare the way for the
moment of awareness when the 'décors s' écroulent' and the
inhabitants are forcibly confronted with their own mortality.
After a while, even the plague becomes a habit for some,

such is the perversity of man's desire for security. You can
get used to anything, Camus's mother used to tell him. The
inhabitants of Oran grow accustomed to the plague, thus en-
abling themselves to avoid the uncomfortable and distress-
ing consequences of thinking about it. Rather than have their
lives disrupted by pestilence, they will adapt to it. 'In the
morning, they harked back to normal conditions, in other
words, the plague.'

The impression of a common experience, which the
reader shares with the narrator and with the inhabitants of
Oran, is further strengthened by a scrupulously objective
style. In a parenthesis, Rieux confides to the reader that he
has deliberately sought to be objective, because he did not
want to distort the truth as he saw it:

> So as not to play false to the facts, and, still more, so as not to
> play false to himself, the narrator has aimed at objectivity. He
> has made hardly any changes for the sake of artistic effect.

The narrator has determined to tell the truth, the whole
truth, and nothing but the truth. Zola wrote that the novelist
should do no more than note the facts, and this is what
Rieux intends in his account. Hence the horrifying details
are related dispassionately for the most part, and the reader
is encouraged to feel that the events described, though ultimate in their horror, are in a way quite ordinary. . . . Moreover, the doctor's style is in direct relation to the clear-
sighted lucidity which Camus claims is necessary if one is to
overcome the Absurd. Rieux uses language for clarification,
not obfuscation as he implies some of his more conservative
colleagues do. Language and style for him serve to sweep
the decks clear of confusing evasions and face the truth as it
is. 'For rats die in the street; men in their homes.' In describing the death of a rat in lurid detail, Camus is setting an
example; it is for the reader to apply this ruthless objectivity
in his contemplation of the human predicament:

> The animal stopped and seemed to be trying to get its bal-
> ance, moved forward again towards the doctor, halted again,
> then spun round on itself with a little squeal and fell on its
> side. Its mouth was slightly open and blood was spurting
> from it. . . .

'What's more, the plague suits me quite well and I see no
reason why I should bother about trying to stop it,' he tells
Tarrou. Hence his second, far worse, crime, which is com-
placent acquiescence in the disaster. He is on the side of the

plague, against its victims: 'Yes, "accomplice" is the word that fits, and doesn't he relish his complicity!'

Camus presents the portrait of Cottard in such a way that we are led not to despise him but to pity him. The reasons for his alliance with the forces of evil are simple and pathetic. He was lonely before, under an individual threat which isolated him. Now the threat is general, 'everyone's in the same boat.' and he can feel the comfort of walking shoulder to shoulder with his fellows. More than anything, he wants human warmth, he wants people to like him, and the plague, a common enemy which erases all previous distinctions, places him on the same level with everyone else. He becomes garrulous and gregarious, mixes with the crowd, initiates conversations. His morbid self-absorption disappears. No wonder he welcomes the plague; it gives him a new lease of life:

> The thing he'd most detest is being cut off from others; he'd rather be one of a beleaguered crowd than a prisoner alone.

Tarrou, from whose notebooks we learn these details of Cottard's behaviour, does not think there is any real malice in his character (p. 216). He blames him for having refused rebellion and sided with the plague, but is ready to forgive him: 'His only real crime is that of having in his heart approved of something that killed off men, women and children.' There is no greater measure of Camus's love and tolerance than this portrait of a man whose actions he cannot condone but is ready to ascribe to fear and ignorance rather than malevolence.

With the waning of the epidemic, Cottard becomes more and more desperate, reverts to his former neurosis, and finally barricades himself in his flat, from which he shoots wildly at the crowd. He kills a dog, and is in turn killed by the police. . . .

UNACCEPTABLE RESPONSES TO THE ABSURD

Cottard is . . . [a] lonely figure, a wine salesman by trade, withdrawn, solitary and distrustful. He has committed an unspecified crime for which he is wanted by the police and consequently lives in fear and apprehension, talking to no one, shut up with his guilt, says Grand. 'He's a man who has something to reproach himself for.' Grand elsewhere calls him 'le désespéré', which gives us a clue to his significance in the story. In *Le Mythe de Sisyphe* Camus listed unacceptable responses to an awareness of the misery of human life—

suicide, despair, acquiescence and resignation (or meta-physical hope). Of these, Cottard is guilty of the first three, and Paneloux of the last. We do not know exactly what the man has done, but it is intimated that his crime was the result, not the cause, of his despair. He was unpopular, unable to achieve contact with other people, misunderstood and neglected. At the beginning of the book, he attempts to kill himself. The only reason this reticent man will give is 'personal problems' *(chagrins intimes)*. He has abdicated to despair in his empty life.

The advent of the plague effects a profound transformation in his behaviour. The glories in it, turns it to his own advantage by selfish exploitation of the situation, grows rich on sordid, petty black-market dealings. . . .

A Non-Christian Moral

The moral to be drawn from *La Peste* is evidently directly opposed to the moral of Christian doctrine, and this opposition is very neatly epitomized in the conflicting views of Rieux the doctor (pragmatic, relativist, concerned with the immediate, humanist), and Paneloux the priest (dogmatic, absolutist, concerned with the future, theist). I said earlier that one of Camus's most engaging qualities was his uncertainty: his thought was constantly alive, constantly evolving, and never afraid to absorb fresh ideas. This must now be qualified. In the matter of religion he never wavered. There is not the slightest trace of any religious feeling in his work. Camus's agnosticism was refreshingly free of dogma. . . . He was in no way a militant or polemical atheist. A clearer definition of his position would be to describe him not as an 'anti-Christian' but as a 'non-Christian'. He would even prefer the order of premises to be reversed, so that Christians were regarded as 'non-humanist'. He did not feel obliged to attack Christianity with violence; he regarded the idea as irrelevant, and its adherents as mistaken. In 1948 Camus was invited by the Dominicans of Latour-Maubourg to deliver an address. In his speech on that occasion, a measured and tolerant account of his position, he declared that since he did not feel possessed of absolute truth, he could not presume to state that Christian revelation was wrong:

> I shall never start from the supposition that Christian truth is illusory, but merely from the fact that I could not accept it.

Again, in an interview published in *Le Monde* on 31 August

1956, he reiterated the point that Christian experience was closed to him. He said he admired the life and death of Christ, but 'my lack of imagination prevents me from following him any further.' I should prefer to call it not a lack of imagination so much as a lack of fantasy. Camus's vision was resolutely earthbound. His position, therefore, was not that of an arrogant crusader, but of a man who spoke from 'outside' religious experience, while still respecting those who were 'inside'. . . . Notice how the portrait of Paneloux is drawn with charity and understanding; nowhere is it suggested that the priest is an evil man, only that he is seduced by the fallacious logic of an erroneous doctrine. Tarrou says that he is a better man than his sermons; Rieux says that Christians are sometimes given to talking in this way, but they do not really mean what they say. Camus is not here questioning the *sincerity* of Christians, but their *clarity.* He supposes that were they to listen carefully to the import of what they were saying, they could not but be appalled. The obstinacy of Christian belief he does not assign to hypocrisy but to the seduction of rhetoric, the beguiling attraction of a rounded, absolute vision which, as in a jigsaw puzzle, provides all the answers. In his address to the Dominicans, Camus regretted that no loud protest came from the Pope against the atrocities of the Second World War. He was told that the Pope had indeed issued an unequivocal condemnation. But, says Camus, he employed the language of the encyclical, which no one understands. The Pope's utterance had been wrapped in the muddy eloquence of abstractions, and no one could be sure whether or not he had even noticed the bloody sufferings of the faithful. Camus reproaches the religious body for protecting itself from the truth by cloaking it in rhetoric. He does not demand any special conduct from the Christian, only that his conduct should at least be no worse than that of a non-Christian. When a Spanish bishop blesses political executions, it is not as a bishop, or a Christian, that Camus condemns him, but as a man.

When we turn from the Christian to the idea of Christianity, we find Camus rather less tolerant. He deplores the pessimism inherent in the Christian view of the world. By what right can a Christian accuse me of pessimism? he asked the Dominicans:

> I was not the one to invent the misery of the human being, or the terrifying formulas of divine malediction. I was not the

one to shout *Nemo bonus* or the damnation of unbaptized children. I was not the one who said that man was incapable of saving himself by his own means and that from the depths of his degradation his only hope was in the grace of God.

. . . Christianity allows for the presence of injustice in the world, which amounts to condoning it. To accept the Christian revelation is to accept that evil, suffering, and death of innocent children are all part of the Divine Plan. 'Truth will flash forth from the dark cloud of seeming injustice.' says Paneloux. Even if God did exist, Camus would still refuse His creation, as long as it included injustice (*Homme Révolté*, p. 76). Moreover, the Christian view of man is a humiliating one; if he is good, it is God who takes the credit for having bestowed his grace; if he is bad, it is his own fault, or the fault of Adam. Humiliating, and also debilitating, the Christian preoccupation deflects the attention of men from their earthly existence, and thereby weakens their resolve to live well.

Camus regards any doctrine or body of belief which claims a monopoly on the truth as totalitarian. Christianity is totalitarian because its revealed truth is absolute and eternal, and demands the adherence of blind faith. As Paneloux said, you must either accept it all or reject it all; there are no half measures. Camus sees no qualitative difference between Christian and Marxist totalitarianism; they are both alike insults to the dignity and integrity of man. And, because they demand such total adherence, absolute doctrines such as Marxism and Christianity are likely to propagate evil rather than dispel it, since they encourage fanaticism and preclude debate. Camus says to the Christians, neither you nor I can alter the fact that the world is unjust, but please try not to add to the injustice!

Camus was not the first, of course, to be perplexed by the intrinsic paradox of Christian belief. If there is a God, He is either omnipotent, as the doctrine tells us, and therefore malicious (because He allows suffering and cruelty in His world), or, if He is benevolent, He is powerless (because He has not made his benevolence effective). He is either cruel or incompetent—He cannot logically be both. Faced with philosophic games such as this, Camus shows his impatience. Such discussions are sterile, he says, let us get on with the business in hand, which is to live the life we have and limit, as far as possible, the potency of evil. In the words of Rieux,

> Since the order of the world is shaped by death, mightn't it be
> better for God if we refuse to believe in Him, and struggle
> with all our might against death, without raising our eyes to-
> wards the Heaven where he sits in silence?

Camus is happy to respect Christians from the outside while
deploring their doctrine, and to seek out and cherish what
he has in common with them rather than what divides him
from them (cf. Rieux and Paneloux). But this, on condition
that they do not allow their absolutism to foster fanatics, and
that they do not spread false hope in a future life. We have
seen often enough that Camus was irritated by the evange-
list encouragement of a useless hope, which he regarded as
an insult to life. [He wrote in *Noces*,] 'If there is a sin against
life, it is perhaps not so much to despair of it, but to hope for
another life, and thus rob oneself of the implacable grandeur
of the life we have.'. . . Camus was not a pessimistic man; he
was a realist who had no time for metaphysical fantasy. He
put the point himself very finely when talking to the Dominican friars who had invited him:

> If Christianity is pessimistic as to man, it is optimistic as to
> human destiny. Well, I can say that, pessimistic as to human
> destiny, I am optimistic as to man.

A HUMANIST WITH A SMALL 'H'

Notwithstanding Camus's distaste for Christian revelation,
he has a faith of his own, which, in the end, is just as irrational. It is a faith in mankind. It differs from Christian belief in that it is firmly anchored to the present and to *this* life,
but otherwise it demands a 'leap of faith' almost as inexplicable. I shall avoid the word 'Humanism' as far as possible,
since Camus specifically disavowed the 'narrow certainties'
of the Humanists, but the fact is that his values are entirely
centred on man, his worth, his potential, his misfortunes. . . .
Dr Rieux announces that his only aim in life is 'to be a man',
and one knows that he considers this the highest goal a man
can attain. . . . The spectacle of a man like Rieux, fighting
against all odds to affirm the dignity of the human presence,
is one to excite Camus's most profound love. Like all great
passions, this love is founded on instinct rather than reason.
If reason were brought to bear, Camus could not assert, as
he does in *La Peste*, that men were only guilty through ignorance. He could not claim that all men were essentially innocent, in direct opposition to the Christian dogma that all

men are essentially guilty. Reason would show that both positions are extreme and untenable. When passion has subsided, Camus remains a convinced humanist (with a small 'h') who always assumes that a person is good and decent until it is proven otherwise. He sees more to admire in men than to despise. . . . *La Peste* shows that if men approach each other in this spirit, they will discover the intense pleasure of solidarity that is experienced by Rieux, Tarrou, Rambert, Grand, in their struggle against the enemy which threatens their common humanity. . . . Everyone is in it together, therefore they look for what unites them; Rieux tries hard to concentrate on what he has in common with Paneloux, and exemplifies better than the priest the commandment that one should love one's neighbour as oneself. Only, the self-sacrifice shown by Rieux, Tarrou, Rambert, Grand, . . . is not accompanied by prayer, nor does it expect a reward. It is motivated by a simple, selfless respect for man, whose nobility is demonstrated in the very courage he displays every day, as he perseveres with a life which can never have meaning. Hence Camus's constant respect for others, for their views, their beliefs, their fears and their failings. They are united in sharing the same absurd destiny. *[Lettres à un Ami Allemand,* p. 73. 'I merely wanted men to rediscover their solidarity in order to wage war against their revolting fate.']

Camus's love of man is finally expressed in the many pages which testify to a real and profound compassion for the vulnerability and loneliness of men, separated from the love of their fellows either by exile (Rambert, Rieux), old age (Grand, and the old people of *L'Envers et L'Endroit),* inability to make contact (Cottard), inability to express themselves (Grand, Camus's mother), poverty, or death. The deaths of the Othon child and of Tarrou are described by a man of real sensitivity. Tarrou and Rieux, though associates, do not manage to declare their love and respect for each other before Tarrou's moving death. Camus knew that a declaration of love was never adequate to its task, and that people were always passing each other, as strangers, for want of the ability, or the courage, to say that they loved. 'Love is never strong enough to find the words befitting it.'. . .

SYMBOLIC INTERPRETATIONS

It is time to approach the matter of *La Peste*'s allegorical significance. . . . There is . . . a literal interpretation, of a city beleaguered by plague, and several metaphorical ones, which frequently overlap and vie for precedence in the grand scheme. For this reason, it is perhaps better to call *La Peste* a 'symbolic' novel, rather than an allegory, since the allegory is intermittent, not constant. Indeed, there is a profusion of symbols, open to a profusion of interpretations.

The first, most obvious, and finally least satisfactory interpretation presents the plague as a symbol of the Occupation. There can be no doubt that Camus intended his book to be a tribute to his colleagues in the Resistance and a powerful image of what it was like to live under the rule of totalitarian occupation forces. . . . In the letter to Roland Barthes (11 January 1955) he states explicitly his intention to depict resistance against Nazism. The parallels are striking. Rieux, Tarrou, Rambert and Grand are Resistance fighters. Cottard is the collaborator. Paneloux's sermons represent the attitude of the Church, which did in fact tell Frenchmen that the German invasion was a punishment for their sins, Paneloux himself could be a tribute to the many courageous Christians with whom Camus fought; the gates of Oran are closed and communications with the outside world suspended, as France was so treated by division. A curfew is imposed. Food is rationed, electricity becomes scarce, and police are more in evidence on the streets. When the plague subsides, there are celebrations, similar to the celebrations which welcomed the Liberation of Paris. Cottard, the collaborator, is hunted down and murdered. The weakness of the analogy is apparent, however, when we remember that war is a result of the wickedness of men towards men, whereas a plague is a natural catastrophe for which men have no responsibility. There is no solid comparison possible between the impersonal cruelty of an epidemic, and the *human* cruelty of the Occupation forces. In Camus's mind, however, the comparison might carry some weight, given his reluctance to recognize that men could be *inherently* cruel.

On the metaphorical level, the plague represents the face of death, in its most extreme, capricious and arbitrary form. It is 'the slow, deliberate progress of some monstrous thing crushing out all upon its path.' It forces the inhabitants to admit, for the first time perhaps, their mortality, and to draw the consequences from this realization. It must be admitted that, in this regard, the symbolism is totally successful. There can be no image more horrific than imprisonment of a whole population slowly decimated by a pestilence which might mean death for any one of them within hours. In such circumstances, one would be bound to reflect. By extension, the plague represents anything which, like death, negates human effort or poisons the joy of living. It is frequently referred to as an 'abstraction', at which times it stands for all that passes the comprehension of men and threatens their happiness. And what is this alienation between men and the world but the 'Absurd' described in *Le Mythe de Sisyphe*? The plague itself does not directly represent the Absurd, but the extreme circumstances it entails provokes the inhabitants of Oran to an *experience* of the Absurd by confronting them, unexpectedly, with death. On this level, too, the symbolism works so well that even the reader is forced to undergo a *pseudo*-experience of the Absurd. This is only another way of saying that the plaque forces its victims to come to terms with the condition of life, not in any superficial intellectual way, but fundamentally. The old asthmatic patient, who hardly appears in the novel, says, 'But what does that mean—"plague"? Just life, no more than that.'

A curious interpretation has been advanced in a much acclaimed book by a psycho-analyst Alain Costes, *Albert Camus ou La Parole Manquante* (1973), according to which the plague represents the silence of Camus's mother, and Rieux's struggle is no less than Camus's long fight against sexual inhibition, occasioned by his mother. If this strikes you as odd, ... there is much more in this book to delight the psycho-analyst.

Finally, there is an interior as well as an exterior infection represented by the plague. This is the power of evil which can take possession of the human heart and make men enter into complicity with the 'exterior' plague. 'This bloody disease! Even those that haven't caught it carry it around in their hearts.' This interior infection gives rise to duplicity, lies, deceit, selfishness, all the ways in which a man may be contaminated and tricked into complicity with a world based on injustice. This is what Tarrou means when he says, 'I had plague already, long before I came to this town and encountered it here.' An interpretation which leans towards the plague as an evil which we all carry within us makes the analogy with the Occupation more plausible. For, by suggesting that there is an inner taint which corresponds to the cosmic disaster of the plague, and which works in collusion

with it, the actions of the Occupation forces are more explic-
able. The analogy is not developed, however, to this degree.
Tarrou is the only character to refer to an 'inner plague', and
he means by this not so much a source of evil as a lack of resolve to combat evil, or conscious failure to do so efficiently.
To revolt against the plague means to deny any temptation to
add to the misfortunes of men and to comfort them in the
miseries which befall them.

La Peste was written during the Second World War, and is
a product of that war. It is written with passion and pain.
Nothing, Camus says, nothing will ever justify the weight of
suffering inflicted upon men, and any ideology, religion or
idea which attempts to do so must be resisted. *La Peste* is an
attack on abstract intellectualism. It is a plea for a halt to the
assumed position, the empty talk, the theoretic compassion,
the laboured 'points of view', a plea for living, in spite of or
even because it is the most difficult enterprise in the world.

The World of the Man Condemned to Death

Rachel Bespaloff

The literary critic Rachel Bespaloff was a professor at Smith College during World War II. Her interpretation of *The Plague* came soon after the novel's publication in 1947. This article, written in 1950, is among the last of the writings of the late scholar.

In Bespaloff's view, all of Camus's work centers around the theme of the death sentence. She claims that he is obsessed with the issue of values from the perspective of man condemned to death without hope for supernatural consolation. Bespaloff believes that this theme informs all of Camus's characters, and in the selection printed here, she applies her interpretation specifically to *The Plague*. Bespaloff traces the characters' responses to the sentence of death, stating that Camus prescribes revolt against the death sentence as the main value of the novel.

There a man takes right away the place his way of facing death assigns him. The mind itself loses its dominion.

Julien Sorel: *The Red and the Black*.

Reduced to its simplest expression, Camus's thought is contained in a single question: What value abides in the eyes of the man condemned to death who refuses the consolation of the supernatural? Camus cannot take his mind off this question. All his characters bring an answer; one has only to listen to them. . . .

What moves us straight away is the integrity of the novel, which wishes to be modest, and eventually succeeds in so being. It is not easy to be honest at a time when nothing else is. The style of honesty has its demands, and Camus could not satisfy them without seeking an answer to the aesthetic problem he had to solve within the limits of his talent. How

Excerpted from Rachel Bespaloff, "The World of the Man Condemned to Death," *Esprit*, January 1950. Translated by Eric Schoenfeld.

can one bring into the field of art a reality which defies the means of art, and recapture through fiction an experience which eludes the poetization of recollection? Camus had to avoid fictionalizing too recent an experience which could be expressed only through the direct testimony of the patient. He therefore kept only the structure of the facts in the symbolic equivalent he substituted for them. The image of the plague, here, is a means of rethinking events, on which, with worn-out indifference, we are already turning our backs, a way of straightening up from under their weight, of gauging them. "War," wrote Saint-Exupery, "is not an adventure. War is a disease, like typhus." In order better to make us feel this, Camus painted disease, not war. Consequently, realistic techniques, which, applied to the historical event, would have been laughable, become legitimate and effective. The objectivity with which Camus describes the epidemic is dependent on the same cryptic and non-naturalistic realism he used in *The Stranger.* Perhaps the use of the term *cryptic* to define a style which is at times sententious and whose transparency appears without mystery, will seem debatable. The multiplicity of meanings and interpretations it suggests, the deciphering it necessitates, certainly seem to remove it from allegory, which always conceals some precise object. Nothing of the sort in *The Plague,* where the scourge sometimes designates the event, sometimes the human condition, sometimes sin, sometimes misfortune.

Camus did not attempt to convey the complexity of the events through the technique of simultaneity and juxtaposition of scenes. To the pulverization of time and space he preferred the concentration of a continuous narration which could keep the tone of a testimony. The difficulty lay in taking up, one by one, through symbolic transcription, the themes of life and death during the occupation, starting from both subjectivity and collectivity. Certainly, the theme of the successive manifestations of the scourge is developed in too linear a pattern, and there is something too schematic in the characters, who synthetize the manifold aspects of the ordeal. One should not forget, however, that the real hero is not the I but the *we* elevated to the dignity of the particular being. Those who went through the ordeal of occupation recognize those situations where, speaking of themselves, they were compelled to say *we* at a time when each lived the *we* in an abyss of isolation and exile. The precarious solidarity which had thus linked people as they faced the catastrophe, and which would not outlive this catastrophe, called for a testimony which would rescue it from history and restore it to ethics. This is the task of the poet. Camus answered this call. He tried to describe an experience which had taken place at the level of intersubjectivity, without using either Jules Romain's unanimist technique or an analytical technique. Giving the humiliated *we* a voice required a form of speech simple enough to reflect the banality of the atrocious, and yet closely knit enough to sustain an insurgent thought. The slightest lack of authenticity would immediately have reduced the *we* to the *they*. A poet-moralist and not a novelist-poet, Camus is not gifted with the visionary imagination which creates myths and worlds. He draws a diagram and leaves it up to us to decipher it.

THE SENTENCE OF DEATH

In one respect *The Plague* seems to us to fall short of the reality it recalls: it has no symbolic equivalent for the humiliation of the suffering inflicted upon man by man. It may seem strange that Camus should have deliberately left aside torture and the demonic attempt to reduce man to the state of a superfluous puppet. But we should not forget that the sentence of death is the central theme of his work. It matters little here whether it is nature, fate, justice, or human cruelty which pronounces the sentence. We know that in his most diabolic inventions man only imitates the tortures of life. In principle, the act of inflicting death without accepting the risk of dying, insofar as it transforms a human being into a thing, lays the physical and metaphysical foundation of torture. Camus thought that, in a sense, the sadistic executioner was less exemplary than the mere executioner. The sentence of death which spurred Tarrou's vocation may seem mild in comparison with the horrors of the plague. Camus had to make us feel that there was no essential difference between the two. It is for the same reasons that Camus depicts man's complicity with the plague with great restraint. The "collaborator" who accepts and invites the plague is anything but a monster: he is a humbled individual, unhappy rather than despicable, who takes refuge in catastrophe in order to escape fear. Camus's attitude can be understood: by identifying war with the plague, evil with illness, he wanted to present a picture of sin without God; and in this perspective, the partisans of the plague are no longer "possessed," but sick. This leads him dangerously to dissolve individual responsibility in the diffuse guilt of life. "What is the plague?" says one of the characters, "it's life and that's all." Having undertaken to fight the will to power, Camus had first to cure himself, through a kind of purification, of the passion of contempt, and to serve his apprenticeship in the new discipline of humility—hence, a tendency to hide baseness from view in order to see misfortune alone. And it is certainly not easy to rid oneself of contempt for man, to resist the impulse which for a century and a half has urged the individual to deify himself or to exalt himself in the guise of humanity, because he can no longer stand himself. Guides and healers, the stubborn heroes of *The Plague* remain subjected to the precariousness which binds them to the *we*, of which they are and want to be a part. In short, attempting to be modest without God, they nurse the supreme ambition of doing without God, without aspiring to become gods.

On the way, they discover the three theological virtues. What is it that sustains Dr. Rieux in his fight against the plague, if not faith, that is to say, beyond reasons and proofs, the certainty that the battle is worth fighting unto death. Where does Tarrou draw the strength to die "a good death" if not from hope, the ultimate unforeseen resource which springs from the death of human hopes. And how does he propose to attain sainthood if not through charity, which he calls "sympathy"? But the three virtues have changed their countenance and bearing; they no longer claim they are daughters of heaven and they acknowledge no other origin for themselves than the passion for earthly life in revolt against death. If God does not answer, if he can no longer be made to answer, man is rich only in infinite patience toward himself. Henceforth, the three virtues will have to rely on that patience alone.

THE REVOLT AGAINST DEATH

Thus, in *The Plague*, Camus's answer to the fundamental question—What value can withstand the death sentence?—is no longer the same as in *The Stranger*. For the exiled *I* whose existence is literally nothing but fall—a fall into the past, into the sin of indifference—the often ignored happiness which wells up with memory, the happiness of being, is the only authentic value. But for the man who starts to struggle, living is not enough. Man regains control of himself in the revolt against death, and henceforth this recovery itself, the good will to begin anew without illusions as to the outcome of the struggle, becomes for him the primary value. To be a man condemned, with and among other men likewise condemned: therein lies our task. For Camus, this is the province of ethics—of the *we* engaged in a desperate venture, beneath a narrow sky darkened by the plague. But Camus wants to base the common effort on individual freedom. We have already noted that he defines freedom through revolt and lucidity—by means of what limits freedom, since revolt clashes with the irreparable and lucidity with the irrational. It is a strange freedom whose motto is: "as if." It has made so many concessions to necessity that it can only act "as if" it were freedom. Camus knows this only too well and admits it: "What freedom can there be in the fullest sense without assurance of eternity?" He has granted himself the only freedom compatible with the world of the man condemned to death. Does it bring nothing but a semblance? If we examine it more closely, we can recognize it as the freedom of Adam and Eve banished from paradise, at the moment when alone and unprotected they assume the burden of their earthly existence. The mutilated freedom of Adam and Eve after the fall is not devoid of love, since it begets the solidarity of this first *we* facing a hostile world. If we examine it even more closely, we recognize the frightening present-day freedom with which we face a future that must be created out of nothing. "The individual can do nothing, and yet he can do everything," said Camus in *The Myth of Sisyphus*. *The Plague* reaffirms the same thing on the level of the "we."

What does the ethic of rebellious acceptance bring to the man who rots in the concentration camps of life? It does not tell him, "You are free," or "Cease your complaints." But through the thickness of the walls surrounding him it hammers the same words into him: *"We* are not resigned to your pain; *we* do not accept your defeat. As long as we are lucky enough to escape the scourge, we shall begin anew; we shall commit our freedom in your stead, and we shall not rest until we have obtained your release." Christianity speaks differently: "Be infinitely resigned," it tells the plague-stricken, for beyond infinite resignation begins faith. "Be infinitely resigned, for in your agony begins the contact with God. You must will the agony which reveals to you the God of love. You must will the uprooting which thrusts you into the divine. This good is your freedom, and this freedom is grace."

We do not propose to pit these two ethics against each other. We do not choose an ethic as we choose a coat. It steals in on us, permeates us, and is already within the walls while we are still arguing about it. The de-Christianized ethic is heir to Christianity in more ways than one, if only because it gives primordial importance to the theme of the sentence of death, which is the theme of the Passion. It began with an act of defiance, and it still must bring about the paradoxical fusion of revolt (in time) and acceptance (in eternity). If this ethic implies, as Camus thinks—but does he really think it?—a renunciation of eternity, it would annul itself by destroying the paradox on which it rests. All the contradictions in Camus stem from the fact that he wants to reduce freedom to the liberty of action in history, while seeking to find "freedom in salvation" through history.

Camus had to find the original link between revolt and ethic. In this sense, *The Plague* makes the task easier, for it calls for united action at a time when danger itself is our last refuge. But, if we make revolt the supreme value, in the name of what shall we condemn the partisan of the plague? It is impossible to extract from revolt anything which would lead us to prefer sainthood to cruelty. Should we conclude that the violent revolt against love, while the saints revolt against evil? But then, beyond revolt, we must set up a value which qualifies and determines it.

CHAPTER 3

Narrative and Structure in *The Plague*

READINGS ON
THE PLAGUE

The Circular Structure of *The Plague*

Jennifer Waelti-Walters

Jennifer Waelti-Walters, the director of women's studies at the University of Victoria, analyzes *The Plague*'s structure. She asserts that the novel (which she refers to by its French title, *La Peste*) draws its strength from its centripetal structure, meaning that it generates power through its circular movement toward the center. Waelti-Walters charts the novel's movement in a series of diagrams, first illustrating the cyclical motion of time and plot, and ultimately positioning Rieux at the center of the narrative. Rieux serves as the connecting figure through whose relationships to the other characters the themes of the novel are developed. Waelti-Walters also contemplates the presence of the silent women of the novel through her structural analysis. Finally, she explores the intertextuality—the interwoven texts—so carefully devised by Camus.

Much has been written about the power of *La Peste*, and the major concern is almost always with the book's moral force. To such an end the critic or commentator examines the thoughts and actions of all the major characters one by one, the predominant images, and the symbolic possibilities of the work; yet a study that pulls all these elements together is difficult to find. And this omission is curious, for the book derives its moral power largely from the centripetal strength of its structure as a novel.

La Peste is structured dramatically in five acts (see fig. 1), with the turnaround, as usual, coming at the end of the third section. The first three sections show the increasing sweep of death and a resulting loss of individuality, from the failed suicide of Cottard to the mass burials in part 3. In contrast,

part 4 deals with resurrection in many forms. The myth of
Orpheus, he who goes to the realm of the dead and emerges
unscathed, is used to underline the scandal of death when
the actor playing Orpheus collapses on stage. Then, although the innocent child dies, his fight is a long one; and
shortly thereafter Rieux and Tarrou are revitalized by their
swim. We must believe that Paneloux dies so that he may be
reborn. Grand recovers. Rats reappear. Then part 5 brings
the necessary denouement.

As in *Le Malentendu,* Camus is using the form of a classical tragedy so that all the cultural baggage of the structure—
a sense of human grandeur and the weight of the daily struggle against fate—may be brought to bear on the absurdity of
the situation in which his characters find themselves. In the
play the friction between Camus's plot and characters and the
expectation created by the form builds malaise and frustration
in the audience. In *La Peste* the pace of the tragedy is not that
of a play, but the sense of doom thus generated adds depth to
Rieux's chronicle. This structure shapes the presentation of
the major theme, death, and cuts directly through the book.

The other themes—love, condemnation, and communica-

FIGURE 1.

Part I	Part II	Part III
Rieux's wife		
Private separations	Public separation	Burial
Illness becomes plague	Remedies:	(1) in ground
First death	(1) administrative	(2) in memory
Cottard	(2) physical	Cottard
	(3) practical	
	(4) religious	
	First sermon	
	Town closed	

Part IV	Part V	
	Town open	
Wrongness of death	End	
(1) *Orpheus*	(1) of separation (final)	
(2) child	(2) separation	
Resurrection	Tarrou's death	
(1) swim	Rieux's wife	
(2) Grand	Cottard	
Second sermon		
Paneloux's death		

tion—are sub-concerns born of the major theme and circle around it in a different formation.

A Basic Cyclical Structure

La Peste has a basic cyclical structure (fig. 2). The plague starts in April of one year, grows with the increasing heat, and weakens as the weather becomes colder, finally disappearing from sight in February of the following year. The circle is not closed, however, because, as we are told in the last words of the novel, the action of the plague can flare up again at any time to start a new cycle of destruction—a cycle whose movement is reinforced by the description of the plague as a flail turning around in the air above Oran and by the whistling noise of which Rieux is frequently conscious as his sensitivity to the situation increases.

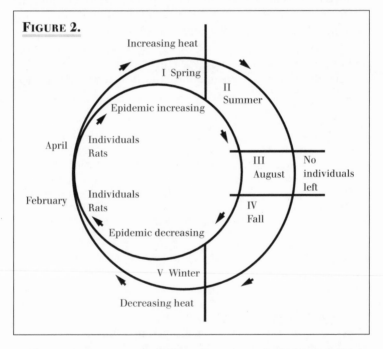

Figure 2.

Increasing heat

I Spring

II Summer

Epidemic increasing

April

Individuals Rats

III August

No individuals left

February

Individuals Rats

IV Fall

Epidemic decreasing

V Winter

Decreasing heat

The circular movement in time is supported by a clearly defined suggestion of geographical centrality if not of total circularity. The city is walled and gated; it sits in the middle of a plateau, surrounded by mountains and sea. Railway lines and marine routes bring traffic in from all sides, and the trams bearing the dead run around the outside edge of the city, along the cliffs. Meanwhile, within it, Rambert, who wants to escape physically, gravitates out from the center to the walls of the city, whereas Tarrou and Rieux, as their friendship develops, move up and in to the high point from where they can see the sea. The crowds mill around in the enclosed space.

Meanwhile the chronicle itself, in an all-encompassing development, starts with a description of individuals (Rieux's wife, Cottard, Michel) and the remedies offered to them, gradually shifts to the group of doctors and their official remedies that are applied to all, moves on to impersonal collectivities (the hospitals, quarantine camps, and mass graves), and finally returns to the individuals who are still alive at the end of the story. Thus a circular movement is created within the narrative itself.

Within this organization of time, space, and narrative, the very characters themselves are disposed in a series of circular structures. We may say that death by plague is the center and that all the characters are concerned with it in one way or another, as illustrated by the grouping of all the major characters around the hospital bed of the dying child. All, that is, except Cottard, with whom we shall deal later, for his absence is indeed part of the structure, as is the absence of active women in the story.

RIEUX IS AT THE CENTER

Most of the characters turn around Bernard Rieux. Each of the major ones shares one of his concerns and usually de-

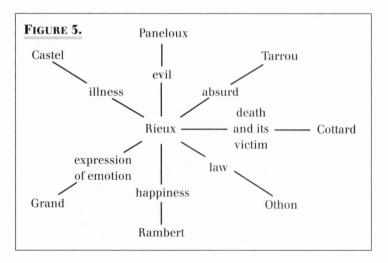

FIGURE 3.

velops it further than he does (fig. 3). Thus Tarrou is linked to Rieux by their sense of the absurd; Paneloux by their fight against evil; Rambert by their desire to find happiness with the women they love; Grand by their inability to express their feelings; Castel by their desire to cure the sick; and Othon by their sense of law and order. In this way the words and actions of each character become part of Rieux's own struggle to act against the plague and to understand it.

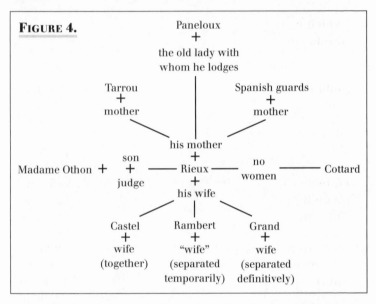

FIGURE 4.

Similarly, the possibilities of the silent relationships Rieux has with his wife and mother are drawn out and explored a little by the relationships given to the other characters (fig. 4). Rieux is separated from his wife. From the scene at the station we learn that all is not well between them. Indeed her illness—tuberculosis—would tend to give a symbolic representation of their relationship for it is traditionally considered in literature to be an illness that strikes a passionate individual and is thus totally opposed to the collective and punitive aspect of plague. . . . We are left with the suggestion that they love each other but that they have not been communicating well. They believe (ironically) that all will be well in the future.

Rambert's separation from the woman he loves, his urgent desire to go to her, and his eventual renunciation of individual happiness in order to struggle for the general good are contrasted directly to Rieux's behaviour. We are left to wonder whether Rieux, too, wishes to join his wife and whether he loves her as Rambert loves his mistress. Interestingly, it is Tarrou, not Rieux, who tells Rambert about Rieux's wife. The doctor himself chooses to talk to Grand. Thus an obvious link is created between Rieux's situation and that of the old man who lost his wife because he omitted to tell her he loved her. Rambert's temporary separation and Grand's permanent one draw attention to Rieux's situation, which is in between; though Rieux thought he and his wife would not be apart for long, he may well lose her before he can express his love to her. Two further developments complete the treatment of the situation: Mme Castel comes back into the city to join her husband, though no one had ever thought that they were a particularly devoted couple, and Judge Othon finds himself lost without his wife, though he was barely civil to her when they were together.

Rieux's relationship with his mother is deep and unspoken; it, too, finds echoes in the lives of the other characters. Tarrou had a silent mother whom he loved deeply and who lived with him until her death. Her memory is the basis for his attachment to Mme Rieux. Rambert finds a surrogate mother in the old Spanish woman in whose house he stays. She looks after him materially, and her comment that he wants to escape for sexual reasons because he does not have anything deeper to believe in touches the crux of his position and helps him decide to stay in Oran. Paneloux also has a surrogate mother in the old woman in whose house he lodges, but his relationship with her is the opposite of Rambert's. He offends the old lady and refuses to explain his attitude and behaviour. She watches over him in silence and finally calls the ambulance in order to do her duty.

Thus the active, thinking men are surrounded by a circle of silent, still, and caring women who are, in effect, absent. There are no active women in the book at all. The young women are not there, and the old, though apparently loving, do not communicate with their menfolk. Whether considered in the context of the absurd or war or evil, this is a curious state of affairs that only becomes apparent when we look at the structure of the novel and that focuses our full attention on the men in the story while binding them more closely together.

An uncharitable explanation of the situation might be that

Camus, faithful to North African customs, French philosophical tradition, and the practice of the Roman Catholic church, did not think of women as either active or thinking beings. (We notice that Paneloux inevitably addresses his congregation as "mes frères," though only the second time are we told that it is a men's mass.) This attitude is certainly explained partially by reference to his own life: his mother was deaf and silent, and he was separated from his wife during the war; hence women were essentially absent from his life and love remained unexpressed.

A CIRCLE OF TEXTS

This almost total silence is particularly interesting, however, when we consider that the men show themselves quite capable of communication (fig. 5). Certainly, it is always a struggle for Grand to find the right words to express himself, but he does finally write his letter to Jeanne. All the others write regularly during the plague: Tarrou keeps a notebook; Paneloux prepares two sermons and does research, as does Castel. Rambert is a journalist and so, of course, he has no trouble in this respect; he is just temporarily prevented from writing by the situation. And Rieux is supposed to have written the chronicle we have read, so we must assume that his silence concerns his personal emotions only.

Again we see that the men are grouped around Rieux, offering us a variety of texts, all of which have something in common with Rieux's testimony: Castel offers medical re-

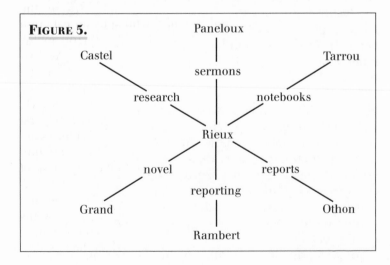

FIGURE 5.

Paneloux — sermons

Castel — research

Tarrou — notebooks

Rieux

Grand — novel

Rambert — reporting

Othon — reports

search; Rambert describes facts in a form intended to interest the public; Tarrou makes observations and personal comments for his private use; Grand goes one step further and expresses his concept of the world as fiction; Paneloux draws theological and moral precepts from what he experiences. Each in his own way offers a description of the plague. Rieux's work incorporates all his friends' forms of writing except fiction, and fiction is, of course, present in the very form of *La Peste.* Hence the male characters circle around Rieux yet again, providing comment on his activity.

Through this recurrence in the structure, the three levels of Rieux's life and action—his struggle against the plague, his feelings, and his writing—are enriched, varied, and called into question by the concerns and actions of the other characters, giving the novel great density of texture.

THE SUBSIDIARY GROUP OF CHARACTERS

The one character who has not been accounted for in all this is Cottard. Curiously enough, he would seem to offer a negative image to Rieux's positive one. Cottard seeks death at the beginning and never fights it; in this way he is for the plague and against Rieux's conception of medicine. He is against the law whereas Rieux is for it, as illustrated in what they do for Rambert. Cottard writes nothing, has no job, no convictions, and no women in his life. He aims only to survive in the crowd whereas Rieux stands alone.

Being the opposite of Rieux is not Cottard's only role in the novel, however. He takes his place with Judge Othon, the asthmatic old Spaniard, and the man who spits on cats in a subsidiary group of characters described by Tarrou in his notebook. Judge Othon interests Tarrou because he, like Tarrou's father, condemns people to death in the name of society; Cottard is the judge's victim. Cottard is a living version of the red-haired man Tarrou saw the first time he went to court. He is a condemned man, and, just as Tarrou followed the first case in the newspaper, so he interests himself in Cottard's activities and reactions. Tarrou's interpretation of his situation in life—that it is impossible to act without taking the risk of being responsible for someone's death—is the root of his interest in all the people around him. The catman is the first person he sees who is probably not hurting anybody by his actions, but he proves vulnerable to changing circumstances and disappears. In the old Spaniard who stays in bed all day,

Tarrou finds a better example of what he is seeking. In his view the old man's repeated actions protect him from all risk of being a judge and possibly make him a saint (fig. 6).

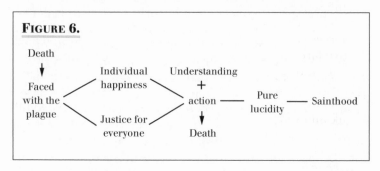

FIGURE 6.

By this subsidiary group Tarrou and Rieux are pulled even closer together. Not only does Tarrou have a place in the group around Rieux, but Cottard and Othon have a role to play in each of the groups. The whole structure is thus rendered more complex, and Tarrou is given preeminence among the men around Rieux. . . .

THE PATTERN OF RECURRENCE

This pattern of recurrence is everywhere in the novel, from Rieux's and Tarrou's daily struggles against the epidemic to Rambert's attempts to leave Oran, Paneloux's two sermons where the second reworks the ideas of the first, Castel's search for an effective serum, and Grand's rewritten sentence to the trains going back and forth to the crematorium and the old Spaniard transferring his peas from one saucepan to another. Every significant action in the novel is done over and over again with the same regularity as the movement of the flail turning above the city.

As we have seen, the group of vocal men and the group of silent women turn around Rieux throughout the novel. The men share his concerns and his activities, and in one way or another they are made in his image. (Indeed all except Grand are described in a similar physical way—solidly built and fairly young.) In this way all their actions direct our attention through themselves to Rieux. The women serve the same function, for they bind the men by a passive bond of silence, separation, and waiting; the mother figures live through their menfolk and suffer for them, the wives are absent. Again figures and context are linked directly to Rieux.

The doctor is therefore the unquestioned center of the novel, and at the end, when he claims to be the voice both of the individual and of the collectivity, he becomes the circumference also. In Rieux himself we find both the structure of the novel and the symbol of that structure; he is the focus of forces emanating from the other characters as well as the active force within the chronicle and the generating force of the narrative itself. The power of *La Peste* comes not only from Rieux's moral standpoint but also from his role within the literary tissue of the work, for never is any element of the book allowed to preempt his presence. The women are all reduced to shadows, and the men are all variations on the main character. The unwaveringly centripetal structure of *La Peste* is one of the major keys to its strength.

The Use of Narrative in
The Plague

Patrick McCarthy

Educated at Oxford and Harvard, Patrick McCarthy
has taught literature and politics at Cambridge, Cor-
nell, and Johns Hopkins University. His book, *Camus*, from which this selection is excerpted, has
been a popular reference for biographical and interpretive information on the French author since its
publication in 1982. In his analysis of *The Plague*,
McCarthy explains that the intricate narrative device
is the key to interpreting *The Plague*'s main themes,
which deal with indifference and the inadequacy or
futility of action.

McCarthy also asserts that another important aspect of the novel is the theme of story-telling itself.
All of the main characters act as story-tellers, weav-
ing their texts through the anonymous overall narrator. Finally, Rieux is revealed as the narrator, apparently giving the novel a conventional form; however,
McCarthy believes that Camus intentionally and
cleverly subverts the narrator's reliability, ultimately
making the novel quite innovative in its use of narrative technique.

La Peste seems such a traditional novel. A plague strikes the
North African town of Oran. First the rats come above
ground to die and then the people fall ill and cannot be
cured. The authorities are helpless and the population despairs. A group of men band together to combat the plague:
Rieux, the doctor who can limit the plague's ravages but can
no longer heal, the mysterious Tarrou, who has crusaded
against the death-penalty, the journalist Rambert, who at
first tries to escape but then realizes he must stay, Paneloux,
the Jesuit for whom the plague is a trial of his faith, and

Grand, the minor civil servant who spends his evenings writing the first sentence of a novel. The group sets up special hospitals and vaccinates people until the plague disappears as suddenly as it has come. Paneloux and Tarrou have died while Rieux is left to tell the story.

Camus stressed that *La Peste* was to be a more positive book than *L'Etranger.* Rieux and his friends demonstrate the moral values of courage and fraternity which do not defeat the plague but which bear witness against it. *La Peste* was read as a parable about the Occupation and Rieux' band was perceived as a group of resistants who are fighting against the overwhelming power of the Nazis. Yet one doubts whether these more positive values represent Camus' main achievement. The outstanding feature of *La Peste* is the way this seemingly simple tale is told and the way in which the narrative technique breaks with traditional novel-writing.

RIEUX AS THE ANONYMOUS NARRATOR

A quotation from Daniel Defoe stands at the head of the book but Defoe's narrators are omniscient; they tell their tales like men who are sure they dominate the world. *La Peste*, however, is recounted by a narrator who flaunts the limits of his understanding. Camus is continuing down the path he had traced in *L'Etranger.* Meursault had tried to understand his life and to communicate its meaning to us. He did not succeed but at least there was an 'I' in the novel. In *La Peste* the story-teller remains anonymous. Not until the end does he identify himself as Rieux; for most of the novel he is a disembodied voice. He too tries to interpret what is happening but the plague defies his attempt to understand and hence dominate it. The opening lines set the tone: 'The strange events which make up the subject of this chronicle, took place in 194–, in Oran. They were untoward and somewhat out of the ordinary, at least in most people's opinion. At first sight Oran is in point of fact an ordinary town, nothing more than a French prefecture on the Algerian coast.'

The precision of time and place is banished by phrases like 'in most people's opinion'. These simple facts are not necessarily true; they depend for their veracity on other unnamed narrators. Nothing is real, Camus is telling us, unless it can be stated by a human intelligence; yet the narrator's intelligence enables him only to speculate without affirming. As if trained in Cartesian logic he draws general conclusions from the specific traits of Oran. But his 'therefores' are soon entangled with 'buts', while his long paragraphs are composed of statements, developments and contradictions. . . .

The inadequacy of the narration cannot be stated until it has been resolved. Then Camus writes of the bond between Rieux and his mother: 'a love is never strong enough to find its own expression so he and his mother would always love each other in silence'. Writing should be a confession; instead it circles around its subject. Free indirect speech—the hallmark of *L'Etranger*—recurs in *La Peste* because it weakens the emotional veracity of the confession. In important moments such as Rambert's decision to stay in Oran, Camus allows his characters to speak directly. Rambert states that he will join with the others to fight against the plague; this is an affirmation of human courage. But such moments are rare because the narration must remain remote.

THE CHARACTERS AS STORY-TELLERS

The theme of story-telling lies at the heart of *La Peste* which abounds in discussions of language and in narrators. First come the official story-tellers like the town government and the newspapers. The government hides reality behind bureaucratic jargon while newspapers console; they keep forecasting that the plague will soon end. Men in authority make bold, ridiculous pronouncements: 'There are no rats in the building,' says the janitor while the rats die all around him. By contrast the theatre offers what Camus might have called 'upside-down' insights. A play is put on and the actor who takes the part of Orpheus is stricken by plague as he descends into hell.

Each of the main characters—Rambert, Paneloux, Grand and Tarrou as well as Rieux—acts as a story-teller and each is a part of the greater anonymous narration. Rambert poses an intriguing problem. A professional journalist, he is the man who should write about the plague. Yet he does not because Camus feels that journalism is a particularly inadequate form of language.

Paneloux, who is an expert on Saint Augustine, delivers two sermons. The first affirms that the plague is a punishment sent by God and that the people of Oran must repent and do penance. This is a traditional piece of rhetoric and Camus uses another story-teller to mock it: Tarrou says that he is waiting for silence to replace bombast. The second sermon affirms that the plague is not sent by God; it is part of an evil which is present in the universe and which the Christian must confront. This sermon is filtered through the scepticism of Rieux who is sitting in the church. He notes that it is heretical but that its very doubts contain some truth. Paneloux' language is more restrained than in his first sermon, while Rieux' language is even more tentative. The second sermon contains some truth because it depicts evil as a painful riddle.

The difficulty which these story-tellers encounter when they start to tell their tales is personified in the figure of Grand. His one-line novel is both an expression of Camus' fear that he will be unable to write and an illustration of the uncertainty of language. Grand puzzles over such words as 'promise' and 'right'; they have a life of their own and they do not convey what he thinks they should. Grand is a frustrated cartesian who would like to make general statements, but when he makes them, they come out as platitudes. 'Never put off until tomorrow,' says Grand. Even then he has to qualify his remark by adding 'as people say where I come from'.

Grand has another aim which is to express fully what he feels. He has been married to a woman called Jeanne whom he still loves. So he wants to write her a love-letter that will make her realize what she means to him. Once more writing should be a confession but Grand cannot find the words to express his love so he sets about his novel instead. One might see in this a parable about absurd art. Language cannot seize human experience directly or totally; it must offer partial insights by 'saying less'. Grand's inability to go beyond the first sentence is a parody of the anonymous narrator's inability to explain the plague.

Tarrou's diary is the best example of 'saying less' and it contains some of the finest writing in *La Peste*. 'Tarrou's chronicle seems to stem,' says the anonymous narrator, 'from a quest for insignificance . . . he sets out to be the historian of things which have no history.' Camus had thought of composing an anthology of insignificance but Tarrou's journal is a substitute for it. Convinced that the world does not make sense, Tarrou describes objects and conversations detached from their context and indicating only the absence of coherence. This seems like Meursault but it is not. Meursault hoped to understand Algiers, whereas Tarrou knows there is nothing to understand in Oran. He asks questions to which he does not expect answers and he spends a page describing the bronze lions on the main square. Irony and brevity are the keys to his art which must surely have appealed to Francis Ponge.

Yet there is a trap in Tarrou's lucidity. Since he knows everything he could become an omniscient narrator, which would contradict everything he knows. In order to preserve the incomplete nature of Tarrou's art Camus presents it via his anonymous narrator who does not understand Tarrou's aim and puzzles over his sentences. He wonders why Tarrou describes the bronze lions; they have no historical or allegorical quality and are just ridiculous objects. Such incomprehension prevents Tarrou's cult of insignificance from becoming an explanation of the world.

As *La Peste* goes on, a tension arises within the narration. In yet another discussion about language the medical authorities shrink from using the term 'plague'. 'It doesn't matter whether you call it plague or growth fever,' argues Rieux, 'what matters is that you prevent it from killing half of Oran.' Language cannot be used propositionally but it can be a weapon. It can combat the plague even if it cannot explain it. So the anonymous narrator turns out, unsurprisingly, to be the plague's chief enemy, Dr. Rieux. If stated at the outset this would have robbed the novel of its remote character; Rieux had to remain anonymous in order to depict the plague as an entity outside man's understanding. But he now states that he has 'deliberately sided with the victims' and that he is 'speaking for everyone.'

THE PARADOX OF ACTION

The gradual change in the point of view is accompanied by a change in the themes. Camus spells out the values which enable men to battle against their condition. The key theme is indifference which is Rieux' special trait. In order to make his rounds and to isolate the people who are infected he has to repress the pity and sympathy which he feels for them. The doctor-patient relationship turns into inadequacy and hatred; the patients hate Rieux because he cannot cure them. But he must ignore this hatred and get on with his work. He feels that he is growing less and less human and that he is as 'abstract' as the plague.

Camus is, characteristically, showing how a destructive force may be creative. The indifference which Rieux feels is a kind of courage which is shared by the men around him. The common bond of courage creates the second value of fraternity. Camus' moral thinking has never been more austere and heroic. Rieux, Tarrou and the others are an aristocracy who sacrifice their personal happiness in order to fight the plague.

The flaw in this moral thinking was pointed out by Sartre and by Roland Barthes. Camus had asserted the need to act but he had not treated the more difficult problems of which action one chooses, how one is changed by it and what influence it will have. Although the plague was non-human, it was supposed to be an image of the Occupation. But the Occupation was far from non-human and it involved agonizing choices. Tarrou illustrates this weakness when he links his stand against the plague with his rejection of violence. Sharing Camus' views on the death-penalty and on left-wing tyranny, Tarrou affirms that he will not kill. So he can combat the plague but he could have combatted the Germans only if one assumes, as Camus did in '43, that the Resistance had its hands clean. Even if one sets aside the problem of the parallels with the Occupation the flaw in *La Peste* remains. Any political or social action would sully the purity in which Tarrou—like Camus—believes.

So the aristocrats of *La Peste* are frozen in their heroic posture. They defy the plague rather as Sisyphus defied his rock and their values are religious rather than practical. This is less a union of men who have very different characters and backgrounds than a communion of indifferent saints whose asceticism has dissolved all character. Tarrou, who broods ironically on sanctity, is writing yet another chapter in Camus' dialogue with his own religious temperament.

Yet these men are not saints, as Camus' Dominican friend, Bruckberger, pointed out. Examining Paneloux' death Bruckberger writes that the Jesuit confronts an absent God in static silence; he does not rail against Him, love Him or live with Him. Grace, love and prayer are all absent from *La Peste*. Bruckberger's criticism complements Barthes': neither the religious notion of grace nor the human virtue of practicality is present in Camus' moral thinking.

The present-day reader may take yet a different view and he may feel that Rieux and Tarrou are exaggeratedly heroic. Indeed Camus' moral thinking is at its best when it depicts the inadequacy of heroism. The dying Tarrou is not content with courage so he turns to Rieux' mother in an appeal for love. Rieux himself is desperately lonely when he walks through liberated Oran at the end of the novel. He and Tarrou are the most masculine of men—tough, ascetic and proud. Yet *La Peste* echoes with the absence of what have traditionally been the values of women: tenderness and warmth. This is far more convincing than the philosophically dubious, uselessly saintly heroism.

The need to present these moral values brings about the gradual change in the narration. At the outset Rieux is a character like Tarrou or Grand and he knows no more than they. Then he begins to show a greater understanding of his friends and of himself. He traces the growth of his indifference and he watches Rambert's hesitations. Meanwhile the anonymous narrator strikes a lyrical note in this description of Oran:

> 'The streets were deserted and the wind sighed out its ceaseless, lonely lament. A smell of seaweed and salt mounted from the raging, invisible sea. The deserted city, white with dust, saturated with briny odours, re-echoes with the cries of the wind and moans like an island of misfortune.'

This is a visionary's insight and it reminds us of the moments of oneness in *L'Envers et l'Endroit.*

THE NARRATOR DISCOVERED

As the novel goes on, the two tendencies—Rieux' awareness and the anonymous narrator's lyricism—increase until they fuse into the discovery that Rieux is the narrator. This makes the novel more conventional because Rieux almost becomes a traditional, omniscient story-teller. Camus tries to prevent this by reverting to the earlier, fragmentary manner but even Tarrou's diary has changed. From being whimsical and insignificant it has become a treatise about insignificance. Camus is grappling with a real problem: there is a thin line between depicting men who show courage in the face of the unknowable and affirming that the world is unknowable so men must show courage. Once one tilts towards the second position then omniscient narrators and traditional novels re-enter by the back door. Camus' language grows more rhetorical and his antitheses—'man's poor and awesome love'— grow heavier.

Yet the incomplete quality of the narration persists to the end. The last entries in Tarrou's journal are puzzling reflections on Rieux' mother and they open a new and mysterious theme of Tarrou's mother. The closing pages of the novel are written in the same remote style as the opening pages. There are celebrations, reunions and dancing; they take place according to some new order which is as undefinable as the old.

Despite the presence within the narration of a moralist, *La Peste* does not really make the world more human or more penetrable than *L'Etranger* did. Anonymity and amputation remain the watchwords of Camus' art. He tried to offer a viewpoint which would be positive [and] collective but the pages where it dominates are conventional, whereas the remote narrator who puzzles over Grand and Tarrou is a superb and thoroughly modern achievement. However, most of Camus' contemporaries did not interpret *La Peste* in this way. Camus, the tragic writer who depicted an alien universe, gave way to Camus, the apostle of brotherhood. This view of his writing, which he himself fostered, helped to shape his life over the next years.

CHAPTER 4

Interpretive Issues: Context and Social Views in *The Plague*

READINGS ON
THE PLAGUE

The Historical Context of *The Plague*

Allen Thiher

As a professor of modern French literature, critical theory, and poetics who has taught at the University of Missouri, Columbia University, and currently at the University of Wisconsin, Allen Thiher addresses the importance of understanding the historical backdrop of Camus's France. Asserting that the novel is an allegory open to interpretation, Thiher insists that one must first understand the environment of France, both before and during the Nazi occupation, in order to establish an initial understanding of the allegory. Thiher examines this environment, contemplating the totalitarian ideologies that were at the forefront of the European public consciousness at the time; he explains the conditions of life under the Occupation, including the reaction of important religious figures and the Resistance movement. Thiher believes that *The Plague* is a commentary on the significance and experience of history.

The Plague is situated in a broad context of intellectual and literary history that, in Camus's review, eventuated in the most important historical realities of the twentieth century: the glorification of the state in the rise of fascism and the perversion of utopian socialism that brought about the modern forms of communist tyranny.

These two historical forms of terrorism, as Camus calls them in *The Rebel*, impinged directly on life in France, and an understanding of both is necessary to grasp one aspect of the referential dimension of *The Plague*. As an open allegory, *The Plague* could be read without reference to Hitler's extermination of the Jews or to Stalin's purge trials. But *The Plague* is a novel about history, and to exclude

Excerpted from Allen Thiher, "Teaching the Historical Context of *The Plague*," in *Approaches to Teaching Camus's* The Plague, edited by Steven G. Kellman. Copyright © 1985 The Modern Language Association of America. Reprinted with permission from The Modern Language Association of America.

these historical events from its field of reference would be a futile exercise. Rather, the most sensible reading is to see first how the novel works with regard to these monumental historical events. . . .

AN OPEN ALLEGORY OF HISTORY

Most immediately *The Plague* appears to demand some knowledge of the French intellectual and political scene before and during the Occupation years of 1940–44. Though Camus had begun thinking of the plague as a symbol before these years and rewrote the novel in large part after the liberation, the Occupation years and their extraordinary history do seem to provide the first test case for finding a referential use for this allegory. . . .

The utterly surprising sudden defeat of the French and British armies in 1940 provides a model for the sudden spread of the plague. Perhaps no one is ever prepared for the total destruction of normal order and for the occurrence of the impossible. In this regard the inexplicable springtime victory of the plague bacillus parallels France's collapse in a few weeks at the hands of a motorized German army that seemingly nothing in Europe could stop. This army arrived in a France that was already acutely divided in its political allegiances: some conservative French citizens were already prepared to accept alliance with Hitler as preferable to continued experiments with a democracy that had allowed communists, socialists, and Jews to govern when the Popular Front came to power in 1936. Other apolitical but unscrupulous French were ready to exploit whatever material opportunities might come their way in the aftermath of defeat. And a large percentage of the working class in France was caught in the curious dilemma of choosing between its patriotic duty and whatever orders the Communist party would receive from Moscow concerning the proper stance to take toward the Occupation. The invasion rolled over a France that had been, moreover, demoralized by poor planning, by its blindness to the nature of Nazi ideology, and by a general military and bureaucratic ineptitude that, for Camus, is the essence of all bureaucracies. Reflections of these multiple confusions find expression in *The Plague*, especially in the administrative hesitations to recognize the true nature of the scourge that has set upon the city and in the administrative caution in the face of an undeniable catastrophe that threatens the lives of all. . . . The open side of the allegory in *The Plague* allows simultaneous readings of history . . . the bureaucratic rationalization at work in the novel could apply to Russia's state apparatus as when, during the thirties, Soviet functionaries organized political machinery that would ensure their own execution. . . .

THE MEANING AND EXPERIENCE OF HISTORY

The Plague is a metahistorical work reflecting on the meaning of history and of human experience as described by history. In this perspective it is no accident that the unnamed narrator of the novel presents himself at the outset as a historian or a chronicler of events or that Tarrou's notebooks are also described as the work of a chronicler. These "historians" wish to write a history that is a record of human resistance to evil and oppression. This use of history stands opposed to the use of history that seeks to justify evil and oppression and especially the acceptance of defeat because that defeat is inscribed in history. In fact, after the defeat in 1940 more than a few collaborators called upon future history to justify their ignominious acts, for they saw themselves as accepting a necessary defeat that future history texts would justify as a product of the inevitable course of events. This future history would have been, one supposes, the future chronicles of Nazis looking back on the New Europe they had created. Opposed to this future history that can be written to justify anything retrospectively is *The Plague*'s imaginary version of present history. This history written in the present and documenting an ongoing struggle against the inevitable, against defeat, pestilence, and death—in short, against the absurd—is the only kind that can justify a people's resistance. It is not unlike the history that might be written by a Russian dissident today or, closer to home, a civil rights worker in the American South yesterday.

The Plague refuses grandiose speculation about evil. Rather it shows that the eruption of the absurd into ongoing history disrupted the patterns of daily life in innumerable ways, some grotesque, some comic. Camus's irony is somewhat caustic in this portrayal, for he has the narrator note that his compatriots' humanism had not prepared them for dealing, in terms of daily needs, with a scourge that goes beyond all human measure (and by choosing the inhuman plague as the image of the absurd, Camus emphasizes the very lack of human measure to this evil). The first result of such an inconceivable disruption of life is that human beings are cut off from one another, isolated behind the walls of prison, of the city, of the armed camps that besiege the land. Camus's choice of the city to portray isolation in *The Plague* is most directly motivated by the historical reality of France during the Occupation: after defeating France the German army first partially, then totally occupied the country, leaving the French with no direct means of communication with the civilized world. Existentially, then, most of the French experienced the Occupation as a period of imprisonment during which one might disappear from one day to the next, arrested by the Gestapo or deported to work as slave labor in Hitler's Reich. (Camus was initially afraid that his name was on one of the deportation lists; the bacillus could strike at any moment with instant results.)

Is Resistance Futile?

Yet, even as men and women are carried away in the night, life must continue with its daily necessities. *The Plague* is perhaps most clearly referential in the way it documents the details of how daily life goes on in the face of an occupying army. The rationing of food, the hedonistic drinking, the re-runs of films in the cinemas, the hoarding of scarce goods and the organizing of a black market, the closing of shops left abandoned by the "departed," the imposing of curfews, the creation of "isolation camps" for mass internments, the inordinate demands made on one's physical stamina—these and many other details offer exact parallels with life during the Occupation. It is only with this sense of the reality of daily routine in a land occupied by the absurd that one can make the next imaginative leap that the novel demands: what can be the meaning of resistance in such daily circumstances in which there seemed to be no hope for the future? For in the early months of the Occupation virtually no one in occupied France believed that the Germans would soon, if ever, be defeated.

Resistance to the occupiers developed slowly in France, starting with the most humble organizing, by very small groups, of ways to disseminate tracts that might keep some hope alive. This experience stands behind the way that in *The Plague* Camus draws back from any suggestion that resistance entails heroics. The history of the Resistance from 1940 until the liberation in 1944 is as much a history of disappointments and defeats as it is a glorious chronicle. Camus wishes to show that in times of calamity the oppressed are obliged to begin slowly their counterattack, with small but constant acts of resistance that demand great patience as well as courage. Fatigue and boredom were also enemies opposing resistance; and in the early months of organizing, Resistance fighters spent countless and what must have seemed fruitless hours in discussing, waiting, fearful hiding, and expending enormous effort for tiny and only symbolic gains. As the Resistance struggle slowly became more militaristic, it also had to take on some of the characteristics of the Nazi occupier: the willingness to lie, to resort to deceit or any other tactic to carry on the fight, and finally a willingness to kill the oppressors and traitors, knowing that innocent victims would later die when the Nazis sought retaliation.

The Resistance offers, then, a primary lesson in how the need to destroy the inhuman has a diabolical capacity to convert virtuous persons into the inhuman themselves—out of virtuous necessity. This motif is found throughout *The Plague*, though perhaps its expression is most fully developed when Rieux must meditate on Rambert's accusation that Rieux is living "in abstraction." Like the invisible plague bacillus, like the great Nazi machine that can only be seen in the individual presence of young German soldiers, evil is an absurd abstraction that kills and, as it kills, obliges resistance to take on its own abstract forms. Though resistance is a necessity, one must never forget that mass executions are also undertaken in the name of virtue. This lesson in ambiguity is the most crucial one that Camus would have us glean from modern history. . . .

Resistance must be undertaken with a full awareness that it can transform itself into an oppressor like the very oppressor that first gave birth to resistance (and the excesses in retaliation that were committed after the liberation in 1944 show that the Resistance movement was hardly exempt from murderous tendencies). Yet the logic of the absurd requires that one make a choice: either one resists or one accepts the absurd presence of evil. As in occupied France, men and women of goodwill must either accept the inevitable as the only reasonable choice or embrace struggle as an absurd leap of faith—in order to defy the absurd. Initially most of the French reacted in confusion to the Occu-

pation, and many felt, as *The Plague* puts it, that there was
no choice but to fall on their knees. In contrast to this acceptance, Tarrou's initiative in creating voluntary sanitary
squads represents the kind of modest resistance to the absurd that Camus proposes; whereas Father Paneloux's sermon, urging the citizens of Oran to accept the plague as a
blessing, represents the attitude of those who not only accept
historical necessity but attempt to convert it into a justification for whatever is.

A REAL DILEMMA

The contrast between Rieux's work or Tarrou's volunteer activism and Paneloux's sermons illustrates a very real
dilemma that the French faced in the Occupation. Many
asked themselves if they should begin a hopeless struggle
against unprecedented evil or if they should make the best
of it, perhaps even finding in this scourge a well-merited
punishment, if not some kind of divine retribution for the
decadence that many French believed had fallen on France
in the twentieth century. Camus's thought on human innocence takes on its full import in the historical context of
France's defeat and occupation. For many French were all
too willing to see in this defeat a sign of their guilt—guilt for
having embraced democratic excesses, for having allowed
chaos to reign or political adventurism to have free course,
or simply for having strayed from whatever these French
took to be the true traditions of the French nation. On both
the right and left sides of the political spectrum one finds at
the end of the thirties a remarkable consensus about
France's decadence. France's defeat could thus be easily in-
terpreted by many as a merited form of punishment for
France's faults, for who was finally guilty of these faults, if
not the French themselves? The logic of guilt seemed only to
demand that one fall before the divine father and beg for-
giveness—and Pétain was more than willing to play this role
of the castigating father of the nation when he became the
leader of the puppet regime established in Vichy. Paneloux's
sermons, especially the first one, set forth an analogous kind
of thought. This priest, a specialist in Augustine, demands
that his followers fall on their knees and repent, recognizing
in the plague a merited retribution for their sins. Moreover,
in accepting what Paneloux calls the "immutable order" of
things, which the reader may take to be God's will or the or-

der of history, the guilty can recognize that evil is really good, for evil leads the guilty back to an understanding that suffering is necessary and hence justified. Echoing in Paneloux's words that justify evil is a kind of masochistic luxuriating in defeat, especially as he describes the angel of the plague to be as beautiful as Lucifer. One hears reverberations of Vichy rhetoric as well as a fascinated admiration of evil, a self-accusatory admiration that many French felt as they watched the blond troops of the conqueror, resplendent in their machine-like order, march unopposed down the Champs Elysées in Paris. Here were angels of Satan that could be taken to be divine messengers, at least by those predisposed to fall down and proclaim their guilt.

Like almost every other element in this open allegory, Paneloux's position points to the political debates that began as the Occupation came to an end and, in those days of uncertain hopes about political reform or revolution, as the French began to debate about the kind of state they wanted to see replace the discredited Third Republic. The emergence of the Communist party as the most powerful political group in the Resistance and the desire for revolutionary change by many noncommunist French meant that a debate about ends and means in politics became a central political issue. It was no idle question, then, when one asked in the months preceding and following the liberation if the communist desire to maximize the eventual happiness of humankind on earth could justify the revolutionary terrorism that the realization of such a goal might demand. Paneloux may be a specialist in Augustine, but his position also recalls the Hegelian theodicy that offers a doctrine saying evil and suffering are necessary in historical terms to produce the final good embodied in the rational state.

Paneloux's sermon would demonstrate that suffering is necessary if divine providence is to be realized. Once divine providence is identified with history, as in Hegel's thought (and, one could argue, in Marx's), then the conditions are ready for what Camus saw as the rational terrorism of the twentieth century: the elimination of all those who oppose the movement of history. Communists believed that the elimination of those guilty of the objective sin of opposing a classless society was justified by the happiness of the greatest number. Intellectuals such as Camus were not so certain that the ultimate goal of a just state could ever justify murder—any more than the miserable death of a child in *The Plague* might be justified by an eternity of bliss in heaven. . . .

A socialist revolution has a rational and ethical plausibility that explains why many French were and are willing to entertain the notion that the ultimate good realized by a just society can justify the imposition of a dictatorship of the proletariat and the terrorism that may accompany this seizure of power. . . .

Political debates of the forties also find expression in the conversation between Rieux and Tarrou. Tarrou gives direct voice to the political views that Camus expressed in the newspaper *Combat* and in other essays of the time: he refuses any political state that depends on legalized murder for its foundation. This refusal is a rejection of the apocalyptic revolutionary ambitions that, unknown to those who have them, are carriers of the plague. But Rieux's reserve toward Tarrou's desire for a kind of sanctity also expresses a recognition of the difficult political and moral choices that the world can impose. It was necessary to kill Germans and fellow French citizens to liberate France. Rieux's attitude toward Tarrou reflects a resigned acceptance that pacifism or the refusal to take life may well not be in harmony with the absurd realities of the world. And these absurd realities had become considerably more complex after the defeat of Nazi Germany.

The Plague was published in 1947. Communists initiated strikes that year against the government in which they were participating as coalition partners, war had begun in Indo-China and was about to begin in France's North African colonies, the socialists were losing electoral strength to the right and to the left, and a year later the Berlin airlift clearly signaled that a new era of power politics had begun in earnest. This was the context in which Camus's novel immediately acquired new meanings, transforming this "chronicle" about the recent plague years into a moral parable about man's possibility for action in a world of struggle for liberation and social justice, of continuing tyranny and repression, though now a world capable of self-annihilation.

Placing *The Plague* in the Context of Camus's Life

David Sprintzen

In this selection, David Sprintzen, who teaches at Long Island University, suggests that in order to fully appreciate the allegorical significance and metaphysical themes of *The Plague,* one must understand the historical and cultural context of Nazi-occupied France, as well as the personal experience of Camus. Sprintzen explains the historical environment of occupied France, supplementing it with a cultural analysis of Oran (which stands as a metaphorical equivalent to France's pre-war Third Republic) as a setting ripe for invasion. In addition to his historical and cultural analyses, Sprintzen explores Camus's life during World War II, demonstrating how the author's personal experiences and observations of war-torn France informed his characters, including their metaphysical concerns. Finally, Sprintzen discusses the plague as a metaphor, arguing that its inhuman nature limits the novel's effectiveness as an allegory.

"With the experience of the absurd, suffering is individual. Beginning with the movement of revolt, it becomes conscious of being collective. . . . The first advance, therefore, of a mind seized by the strangeness of things is to recognize that it shares this strangeness with all men, and that human reality . . . suffers from this distance from itself and from the world. The pain [*mal*] which was experienced by a single man becomes a collective plague" (L'HR, 36; R, 22). Could Camus have been more explicit about his intention? The transition from *The Stranger* to *The Plague* turns upon the emerging perception "that all . . . were, so to speak, in the same boat" (P, 61). The imprisonment of Meursault has become the shared experience of the citizens of Oran, who are often referred to as "prisoners of the plague." In fact, at an early stage in the development of the manuscript, Camus had considered calling it "The Prisoners."

A concern with imprisonment runs through his writings, and with good reason. With *The Plague*, the metaphor of prison helps to transcribe the traumatic experience that was the German occupation of France during World War II. At a deeper level, however, the continuity with the stage of the absurd is maintained by the recognition that in prison our life is finite, time and space are circumscribed, and our liberty of action is constrained by forces beyond our control. . . .

It is important to note four complementary perspectives from which the novel can be viewed: the personal, the historical, the cultural, and the metaphysical. By considering these dramatically interwoven thematic strands, the sensuously textured tapestry that gives experiential richness to the sparse contours of the chronicle of the plague can be more adequately appreciated.

A PERSONAL AND HISTORICAL CONTEXT

At its most obvious, "*The Plague* . . . has as its evident content the struggle of the European resistance against Nazism" (TRN, 1965; LCE, 339). It also had its quite personal accent, for Camus was quite literally trapped in occupied France. Rambert essentially transcribes the qualitative feel of this experience, in which Camus found himself cut off from his wife, his family, and his native Algeria when the Allies invaded North Africa. Camus's feelings during his recuperation in the mountains of central France from an attack of tuberculosis must certainly have been echoed by Rambert when the latter exclaimed that "his presence in Oran was purely accidental, he had no connection with the town and no reasons for staying in it; that being so, he surely was entitled to leave" (P, 77). As Rambert so poignantly exclaimed, "I don't belong here!" If most people in occupied France felt deprived of their right to live in accordance with their normal habits and expectations,

> those . . . like Rambert . . . had to endure an aggravated deprivation, since, being travellers caught by the plague and forced to stay where they were, they were cut off both from the person with whom they wanted to be and from their homes as well. In the general exile they were the most exiled;

since while time gave rise for them, as for us all, to the suffering appropriate to it, there was also for them the space fac-
tor; they were obsessed by it and at every moment knocked
their heads against the walls which separated their infected
refuge from their lost homes (P, 67; TRN, 1236).

Still more, there is "the case of parted lovers," which includes Rieux and, in another sense, Grand. There was "the
trouble they experienced in summoning up any clear picture of what the absent one was doing," and of reproaching
themselves for having paid too little attention to the "way in
which that person used to spend his or her days" (P, 68).
"Thus, each of us had to be content," writes the narrator, "to
live only for the day, alone under the vast indifference of the
sky. This sense of being abandoned, which might in time
have given characters a finer temper, began . . . by sapping
them to the point of futility" (P, 68). The year or so immediately following the Allied landing in North Africa, it might be
noted, was certainly not a particularly happy or productive
one for Camus.

Camus had resented the war from the outset. It did not
make sense to him that such extraneous events, with no direct
or perceptible relation to his life and his personal and philosophical concerns, could so wrench him out of his orbit. . . .

The initial dialogue between Rambert and Rieux concerning Rambert's desire to get out of Oran might have taken
place within the soul of Camus. Rambert comes to this discussion with "the sulky, stubborn look of a young man who
feels himself deeply injured." Rieux "wished nothing better
than that Rambert should be allowed to return to his wife
and that all who loved one another and were parted should
come together again." He recognized that Rambert didn't belong here, but said, "That's not a sufficient reason. Oh, I
know it's an absurd situation, but we're all involved in it, and
we've got to accept it as it is."

Rambert is bitter. "'You're using the language of reason, not
of the heart; you live in a world of abstractions.'" To which
Rieux responds that he "was using the language of the facts as
everybody could see them—which wasn't necessarily the
same thing." Rambert "was right in refusing to be balked of
happiness. But was he right in reproaching him, Rieux, with
living in a world of abstractions? . . . Yes, an element of abstraction, of a divorce from reality, entered into such calami-
ties. Still, when abstraction sets to killing you, you've got to get

busy with it" (P, 78–81). The concern with happiness has clashed with the hard facts of life as well as with the role of abstract forces in structuring that "force of evidence" with which one must come to terms. We thus see dramatically transcribed a deeply personal conversion from the individualism of the Absurd to the emerging theoretical concern with solidarity that is so central to the stage of Revolt.

Only slowly did Camus come to terms with his own situation, resume his writing, and make contact with resistance forces, most particularly the Combat network. Ultimately he became the chief editor of the underground network's newspaper, *Combat*. This position, when made public upon the liberation of Paris, contributed significantly to his becoming a major public figure in postwar France. In much of this, the resemblance to Rambert is close—though far more as a transcription of feeling than of action.

Camus did, however, deepen his appreciation of the efforts of ordinary people to make sense of their life, faced with a daily routine that leaves little place for imagination and hope. No doubt his own origins among the poorest of French North Africans left him with a profound respect for the quiet dignity of those whose condition does not let them aspire beyond the simple pleasures eked out from, and the silent sufferings endured within, the daily struggle for subsistence. In such circumstances, simply doing one's job may embody nobility. . . .

"'Oh, doctor,'" exclaimed Joseph Grand, that nondescript clerk in the municipal office who "had suffered for a long time from a constriction of the aorta" (P, 17), "'how I'd like to learn to express myself!'" (P, 43). If only he could "find his words" he would be able to tell his lost love, Jeanne, what he feels. It would be "hat's off," and he could achieve that minimal acknowledgment that would reconcile him to his life. Throughout the turmoil of the plague, Grand sticks to his work in the municipal office, while working with the sanitation teams in off-hours, and in the evenings continues his project of writing the perfect novel.

"'There lies certainty,'" observes Rieux, "'there, in the daily round. . . . The thing was to do your job as it should be done'" (P, 38). Yet the routine of such a life tends to wear one down. "'Oh, doctor,'" Grand exclaims somewhat later, "'I know I look a quiet sort, just like anybody else. But it's always been a terrible effort only to be—just normal'" (P, 237).

In his ability to continue at his work with care and concern for others, in the shadows of anonymity, Grand incar-
nates Camus's sense of the nobility of the ordinary. "In short,
he had all the attributes of insignificance" (P, 41). No doubt,
it is this that Camus wishes to celebrate by having Rieux observe that "Grand was the true embodiment of the quiet
courage that inspired the sanitary groups," and, thus, "if it is
a fact that people like to have examples given them, men of
the type they call heroic, and if it is absolutely necessary that
this narrative should include a 'hero,' the narrator commends to his readers . . . this insignificant and obscure hero
who had to his credit only a little goodness of heart and a
seemingly absurd ideal" (P, 123, 126).

It was in order to bear witness to the intrinsic nobility of
the efforts of the average person that Rieux (and Camus) "resolved to compile this chronicle . . . so that some memorial
of the injustice and outrage done to them might endure; and
to state quite simply what we learn in a time of pestilence:
that there are more things to admire in men than to despise"
(P, 278). In this, Camus uses Rieux to express one of the
more profound sources of his art: the felt obligation to give
voice to those whose quiet dignity speaks loudly in action
and in suffering, but who cannot find their own words with
which to do it justice. From this source, Camus feels, artists
can draw creative and vitalizing energy, as well as a justification of their work.

ORDINARY ORAN: BUSINESS AS USUAL

But if, through the person of Grand, Camus wishes to pay
tribute to the quiet courage displayed by his compatriots
during the occupation and in the Resistance, and by most of
the world's poor and working people in their daily effort
"just to be normal," his attitude toward the behavior of his
fellow Frenchmen is more complex. They certainly did not
deserve what befell them, but they were not without responsibility for it. In fact, on this nuanced perception of their
complicity in the pestilence-occupation hangs the deeper
meaning of this tale and its place in Camus's work. What
was it about Oran or about the Third Republic that made it
the appropriate host?

Why Oran? Why this "treeless, glamourless, soulless"
town that seems restful but puts you to sleep? (P, 5). In 1939
Camus had called it a spiritual desert, "without soul or re-

sources" (LCE, 111). "Compelled to live facing a glorious landscape," he wrote then, "the people of Oran have overcome this formidable handicap by surrounding themselves with extremely ugly buildings" (LCE, 116). Their "statues are both insignificant and solid. The mind has made no contribution to them, matter a very large one" (LCE, 125), "while the streets of Oran reveal the two main pleasures of the local young people: having their shoes shined, and promenading in these same shoes along the boulevard" (LCE, 113). Little wonder that "the Oranais are devoured by the Minotaur of boredom" (LCE, 116). "'To be nothing!' . . . Without knowing it, everyone in this country follows this precept" (LCE, 131). With the forces of nature in possession of the spirit of the town, one is at times tempted "to defect to the enemy! . . . to merge oneself with these stones, to mingle with this burning, impassive universe that challenges history and its agitations" (LCE, 130). . . .

"The truth is that everyone is bored," notes the narrator, "and devotes himself to cultivating habits. Our citizens work hard, but solely with the object of getting rich. Their chief interest is in commerce, and their chief aim in life is, as they call it, 'doing business'" (P, 4). It is not that the citizenry of this mythologized version of the Third Republic are evil or malicious; they don't aspire so high. "What they lack is imagination. They take their place in the epoque as if at a picnic. They do not think on the scale of pestilences. And the remedies which they imagine are hardly adequate for a head cold" (TRN, 1948). "Really, all that was to be conveyed was the banality of the town's appearance and of the life in it. But you can get through the days there without trouble, once you have formed habits. And since habits are precisely what our town encourages, all is for the best" (P, 5).

And what was the pervasive character of the experience through which they lived? Preoccupied with their practical concerns and their personal satisfactions, they took life for granted.

> In this respect, our townsfolk were like everybody else, wrapped up in themselves: in other words they were humanists: they disbelieved in pestilences. A pestilence isn't made to man's measure; therefore we tell ourselves that pestilence is a mere bogey of the mind, a bad dream that will pass away. But it doesn't pass away, and from one bad dream to another, it is men who pass away, and the humanists first of all, because they haven't taken their precautions. Our townsfolk . . .

went on doing business, arranged for journeys, and formed views. How should they have given a thought to anything like plague, which rules out any future, cancels journeys, silences the exchange of views. They fancied themselves free, and no one will ever be free so long as there are pestilences (P, 35).

"It will be said, no doubt, that these habits are not peculiar to our town; really all our contemporaries are much the same. Certainly nothing is commoner nowadays than to see people working from morn till night and then proceeding to fritter away at card-tables in cafes and in small-talk what time is left for living. . . . In other words [Oran is] completely modern" (P, 4). The Oranais have lost contact with passion, love, nature, and art. Habit rules the day, under cover of propriety, in the service of business. No wonder that the primary concern of the officials is to hide the reality of plague: to deny the evidence, to reject the possibility, and above all to avoid taking any extraordinary measures—even precautions to preserve the public's health—that might interfere with doing business. "'Take prompt action if you like,'" says the prefect, "'but don't attract attention'" (P, 44). Nor is it any wonder that into this world of the everyday, plague entered with such devastating force: destroying routine, undermining habit, separating people, and rendering vain their normal hopes and expectations.

All this had, of course, its educational side. Being cut off from the future, the people of Oran found themselves thrown back upon their personal resources. They were forced to attend to the present with a heightened sensibility to the most minute details. No longer able to take tradition as a self-evident guide to action, they had to reconstitute their sense of the meaningful. . . .

At a more general level, the social order was put, as it were, to the metaphysical rack. Values had to be forged, and personal relations too, into the teeth of a much constricted sense of time. This need for a "transvaluation of values," to borrow a phrase from Nietzsche, was lived by each and every citizen in the crucible of a very personal suffering. Thus emerged the sanitary squads—at first, simply to aid the citizens in combatting the plague. Slowly, almost imperceptibly, they began to resonate communal values, like the resistance movement itself, pointing toward the need for a social and political transformation whose outlines remain unclear. Before attending to these constructive possibilities, let us explore more fully the cultural ramifications of the life of the Oranais.

Oran is a thoroughly bourgeois town. And it is the quality of its social life that constitutes the dramatic setting for the invasion of the pestilence.

Having cut themselves off from nature and from one another, the citizens of Oran have succeeded in reducing passion and spirit to the habitualized pursuit of material success and physical satisfaction. Care and concern for others, for the quality of public life, or for the possibilities of human excellence, have simply been lost in the shuffle. There is no sense of the deeper significance, the "sacredness," of the everyday. Rather than seeking to "exhaust the field of the possible," habit and routine have become the order of the day; propriety its rules and regulations; diversion and leisure its sustaining satisfaction; and material success its aim and crowning achievement.

The forces of dehumanization may thus be said to have crept into the hollowed core of bourgeois society long before the arrival of plague. With its public life so pervaded by the concern with doing business, personal relations inevitably suffer. Concern for others and for the collective well-being cannot compete for attention with business or pleasure. Naïve faith in material progress—guided perhaps by the unseen hand of the market—that has so marked modern bourgeois society, leaves little place for collective efforts to shape our destiny. The human community is thus desensitized to human values and lacks direction and purpose. It is thus that plague might be said to have already crept into the life of this mythologized Third Republic, its presence so pervasive and "natural" that the people could not recognize it. In a sense, they were already the unwitting and even innocent carriers of the germ. With their resistance to the forces of dehumanization so weakened, their personal relations so desensitized, and their sense of the human collectivity so attenuated, they were well-prepared to receive in full force the invasion of this most virulent and destructive pestilence. . . .

COLLABORATING WITH THE ENEMY

Cottard is the only one of Camus's characters who welcomes the plague and anguishes at the prospect of its coming to an end. Yet there is sympathy in Camus's portrayal of him, for he too suffers the yoke of separation and yearns to belong.

Wanted by the authorities, who are closing in on him at the onset of the plague, Cottard suffers from his isolation from the community and fears incarceration above all. In desperation he attempts suicide, only to be rescued by Grand, out of simple compassion. "I can't say I really know him, but one's got to help a neighbor, hasn't one?" (P, 19).

As plague occupies Oran, the authorities' attention is diverted, freeing Cottard from the daily pressures of being under suspicion. He relaxes, becomes humorous and friendly, and begins to feel at home with others. "Say what you like, Tarrou, but . . . the one way of making people hang together is to give 'em a spell of plague" (P, 175).

None of this impedes his ability to traffic in the plague's underground, making money through the black market and off the suffering of others. But without maliciousness. He is merely doing what he knows best. He lives well, but is not without concern for the well-being of others. Perhaps he simply lacks the imagination to conceive of the consequences of his actions. Here he would not differ greatly from most of what could now be called his fellow citizens. The same is true for the authorities—a feeling that well represents Camus's sense that most collaborators in wartime France were primarily guilty, not so much of evil as of a failure of imagination. It may even be said more generally of Camus—as we have noted with Rieux and Tarrou—that he does not see as much evil in mankind as narrowness of vision, self-preoccupation, venality, self-interest, and above all an inability to appreciate the meaning and consequences of one's actions.

Cottard thrives along with the plague. Of course, *that* is his condemnation: to feel at home in a situation that is wreaking havoc on the community. He is thus in league, albeit not viciously, with the forces of inhumanity. He even profits from their occupation of Oran. It is not surprising, therefore, that a growing sense of anxiety and ultimately panic grips him as the plague recedes. As the state of siege is lifted, the authorities will be free to turn their attention to hunting criminals. This "man who hated loneliness" is once again overwhelmed by the fear of being cut off from the community, not realizing that his fate is an inevitable result of a lifestyle that exists at the expense of others. Nor does he seem able to do otherwise. Camus does not explore how Cottard became the way he is. His actions during the plague

seem natural; criminality seems to be his nature, redemp-
tion beyond his ken. The significance of this portrayal of
criminality is not completely clear.

LIMITATIONS OF THE PLAGUE AS A SYMBOL

It is noteworthy that we do not get any comprehensive presentation of the forces that collaborated with the plague. It is
difficult to envisage active support for the plague—however
much Cottard may be taken as one who welcomed it and
benefited from it—because it is difficult to defend the
plague's reign. This is a key limitation of Camus's mythic
transformation of occupied France.

What, it might be asked, is the material base that facili-
tated the plague's entry into Oran, so abrupt and pervasive?
It is almost as if a fifth column were already at work within
the city, perhaps in the form of authorities who unduly de-
layed taking the appropriate measures. Where are the representatives of the business establishment who, during the
Popular Front, proclaimed, "Better Hitler than Blum"?
Where are the internal forces of fascism? The members of
Action Française? The supporters of a renascent French patriotism and anti-Semitism? Those who made it impossible
for France to come to the aid of the embattled forces of Re-
publican Spain? In short, where is the class struggle? What
was the social and class base of the opponents of fascism?
From what segments of society did the resistance draw most
of its strength? And where was the grand bourgeoisie while
the underground network was being developed? Unfortunately, Camus does not address these questions.

By mythologizing the resistance as a drama of the human
condition, Camus's work gained in metaphysical scope and
in internal development. But he pays a serious price at the
level of historical and theoretical applicability. That is partly
the result of his choice of metaphysical symbol. The plague
is a microbe, a force of nature that strikes at the human
community. But it is not a human force, not even primarily
carried by humans. How could human beings identify with
and justify its rule as a social strategy? How could anyone offer it as a solution to the drama of the absurd, as a response
to the need for moral regeneration, renewed patriotism, and
social reconstruction, or as a legitimate way of keeping social order and peace? . . .

In sum, this mythic frame does not adequately allow Camus to pose the problem of human evil any more than it does justice to questions of social policy, political opposition and dissent, class conflict, and social antagonisms in general. That Camus sensed this may be seen from the further development of his work. Nevertheless, it is important to underline the extent to which revolt and resistance are short-changed in *The Plague* if we are to be able to appreciate both the nature of Camus's development and the kind of critical scrutiny he was increasingly to face. In this work we are left with only Tarrou's reminiscences, without any clear sense of the political issues that so fiercely divide equally sincere human beings, leading some to see murder as not only acceptable but often necessary and justifiable.

In his response to Roland Barthes, and earlier to Sartre and Jeanson, Camus failed to pick up the deepest sense of the criticism. He is certainly right when he insists upon the explicit thematic development of his work. "Compared to *The Stranger, The Plague* does, beyond any possible discussion, represent the transition from an attitude of solitary revolt to the recognition of a community whose struggles must be shared. If there is an evolution from *The Stranger* to *The Plague*, it has moved in the direction of solidarity and participation" (LCE, 339). There is, however, another more subtle message that operates at the level of what might be called stylistic metaphysics. Here the commitment at the core of the emerging response to the plague has been so devoid of specific historical and political content—in the service, perhaps, of the mythologized enactment of the human condition—that its message goes little beyond eternal vigilance and mutual respect and solidarity in the face of recurring threats to human living. But where should we look for these threats? Are there no important differences between the dangers of human evil and natural disaster? . . .

Nevertheless, *The Plague* has made clear the need for the establishment of a shared consciousness of our common condition as the precondition for the development of a human community. The entire movement of Camus's thought leading up to and including the novel has revealed the importance, nay, from a social standpoint, the necessity, of such a development. From this perspective, *The Plague* clearly represents a development that finally brings to the fore our collective condition and, by so doing, suggests the framework for a solution to the tragedy of "The Misunderstanding" and *The Myth*. Yet the question of revolt still lacks satisfactory articulation. Revolt has achieved the social dimension hinted at in "Caligula," the recognition that individuals insist upon a certain dignity; that we must establish a communal framework of shared perceptions and meanings if we are to live a meaningful and fulfilling life in the face of a condition that denies humanity; and that there is an essentially communal base to living that must be reflectively grasped as the precondition of constructive human action. This transition stage *The Plague* has clearly established.

But if the social dimension is so essential, what happens to revolt when that dimension itself becomes oppressive? The universe of *The Plague* is Manichean: the good of communal revolt against the evil of the plague. The meaning of the struggle is grounded in the human values that emerge in, and are attested to by, the struggle. But what happens when the oppressive element is similarly human? When, as Tarrou claimed, it is the human being who carries the germ within him? Or when, further, it is humans that deny humans? How does revolt emerge there? And, more difficult still, on what does it seek to base its claims? Construct its community? Where then are the meanings and limits of the endeavor to be found? On these questions *The Plague* offers little assistance. It will be the task of the works that follow to address them.

Dark Night and the Coming of Grace

Bernard C. Murchland

Father Bernard C. Murchland once taught at Notre
Dame University and served as the editor of *Fides*
magazine. In this selection, Murchland charts the
evolution of the author's work, starting with Camus's
early concerns of the suffering of the individual, and
concentrating on the later emphasis on positive social action (as suggested by *The Plague*). To Murchland, Camus's work evolves from a negative type of
existentialism to a positive liberal humanism that
celebrates the potential of humanity. Representing a
popular Christian view of Camus, Murchland ap-
proves of this movement, lining up with Camus in
his break from Sartre, who, he argues, typifies the
negative aspects of existentialism.

When the Nobel Prize for literature for 1957 was awarded to
Albert Camus, a singularly dedicated man of our century was
honored. Both as an artist and a man the outstanding characteristic of M. Camus is his total and tortured involvement
in the world of his time. He is concerned with the intellectual,
political, and moral climate in which we live. He questions
traditional values, the future of mankind, and explores at
great length the conditions necessary for human living today.
"What meaning can be salvaged from the world?" is the rest-
less question that runs through Camus's plays, novels, essays,
and journalistic writings. "We are at the extremities now," he
writes of modern man's plight. "At the end of this tunnel of
darkness, however, there is inevitably a light, which we already divine and for which we have only to fight to ensure its
coming. All of us, among the ruins, are preparing a renais-
sance beyond the limits of nihilism."

The positive quality this passage signals is essential to an

Excerpted from Bernard C. Murchland, "Albert Camus: Rebel," *The Catholic World*,
vol. CLXXXVIII, no. 1126, January 1959.

understanding of Camus's work. There is a temptation for
those only vaguely familiar with his writing to associate him
with a rankly negative school of existentialism, to class him
(with Sartre and others) among the philosophers of the absurd and nihilism. This is particularly true, I believe, of the
American public. An article in one national review awhile ago
very unfairly referred to him as "a man of childless thought."

Camus himself, on several occasions, has endeavored to
correct this accusation. In an interview with the French
press he said:

> When I ask what is deepest in me, I find that it is the desire
> for happiness. I have a great interest in people. I have no con-
> tempt whatsoever for the human race. I believe that one can
> feel proud to be a contemporary with so many men of our
> times whom I respect and admire. . . . At the heart of my work
> there is an invincible sun. It seems that all this does not con-
> stitute a particularly sad outlook.

THE ABSURD CRISIS OF THE INDIVIDUAL

. . . In *The Stranger* (1942) and *The Myth of Sisyphus* (1942),
(as well as another play called *Cross Purpose,* published in
1944), Camus attempts to conciliate his obsession with the
absurd and his mystique of sensual happiness. (He had gone
to Paris in 1940 where the slaughter of World War II and his
active role in the resistance were experiences that deepened
considerably his earlier experience of illness.) These works
explain each other and are concerned primarily with the crisis of the individual, with man as a lonely exile struggling
for happiness and meaningfulness beneath the immense
and senseless burden of existence.

The Myth of Sisyphus, the first of Camus's two important
philosophical essays, reveals a new depth in Camus's own
thinking. The question raised in the beginning of this book
is: how can a life that has no meaning best be lived? Camus
considers the possibility of suicide and writes that "it is the
only truly philosophical problem." In the context of this discussion he examines what he calls the "absurd walls" within
which the drama of our human condition is played out. The
sentiment of the absurd is "a light without radiance," which
can strike anywhere at any moment. The banality of daily
life is quite as effective in bringing about its emergence as
the disaster of global warfare. The rhythm of abstract, de-
personalized, uncreative activities crumbles into absurd
chaos before the question: what does it all mean?

Infirmity, ignorance, irrationality, nostalgia, the impossibility of distinguishing the true from the false, our radical inability to know ourselves or others, the implacable mystery of the world—these are some of the elements of the absurd as Camus envisioned it at this time. It was the sum total of all the antinomies and contradictions man is heir to, compounded by the conditions of World War II and Camus's personal experiences. Reason can do very little to introduce motives of hope, unity, and harmony. Religion is even more impotent. The logic of absurdity concludes to the necessity for suicide. But at this point Camus revealed his positive genius. To take one's life would be, in the final analysis, an act of cowardice, of bad faith. We simplify the problem by avoiding it. We must live if we wish to maintain what we believe to be true. "To live is to make the absurd live," says Camus, "To make it live is, above all, to face it squarely. Unlike Eurydice, when we avert our gaze, the absurd dies. Thus, revolt is one of the few philosophical positions." It is in this perspective that Camus introduces his courageous metaphor of Sisyphus. Like the mythical hero, man must accept the limitations of his condition. He must accept absurdity with lucidity and conquer it through sincerity and loyalty.

A SENSE OF UNIVERSALITY

Sometime between 1942–44 Camus reached a new level of development. In his four *Letters to a German Friend,* he proclaims: "I continue to believe that this world has no superior meaning. But I know that something in it has meaning: it is man, because man is the sole being to insist upon having a meaning." Camus's vision now expands to include the suffering and unhappiness of all mankind.

This sense of universality goes considerably beyond the struggle of the individual Sisyphian character in *The Plague* (1947) and *The Rebel* (1951)—another fiction-philosophical combination at a new level of significance. In these two powerful works (perhaps Camus's best) the values of justice, loyalty, and courage appear much more positively on the frontiers of the absurd, values that are as indisputably authentic as they are adamantly anti-Christian. Camus has never wavered in his atheism. Christianity has always appeared to him as another of the pointless ideologies in the name of which men are subjugated and massacred. He has excluded it from his vision as a matter of principle.

The Plague permits of several interpretations. It is first of all the record of a physical epidemic, of a city besieged by some uncontrollable disease which strikes down the innocent and outflanks all efforts made to curb it. In another sense, it is a chronicle of World War II, the war of the occupation and imprisonment of some two million Europeans. The tragedy of Europe is transplanted to Oran and reduced to artistically manageable proportions. At still another level, *The Plague* reaches a note of impressive depth in its concern with the presence of evil in the world. There is, finally, a moral dimension—something new in Camus—introduced in the person of Tarrou. With him, the theme of moral evil, the evil that men inflict upon each other, reaches its greatest intensity. Through Tarrou, Camus's own ideas of commitment, dedication to the plight of others, and courageous stand against violence and injustice are made clear.

The Myth of Sisyphus was concerned with the problem of suicide. In *The Plague* Camus substitutes this problem for that of a strange form of martyrdom, a kind of religion of happiness through atheistic sanctity. (The problem of absurdity is reduced to Tarrou's question: "Can one be a saint without God? That is the only concrete problem I know of today.") But there is in this new emphasis an undeniable deepening of Camus's thought. He has gone beyond the exterior manifestations of absurdity to recognize the reality of spiritual death in the world. The root of absurdity is within us. When Tarrou dies in the presence of Dr. Rieux (who narrates the story), we witness an outstanding example of disinterested love—one of the high points of modern literature. Here Camus realizes that there is no harm in being happy. It is only being happy alone that cannot be justified. This sense of solidarity, based upon sacrifice and personal responsibility for the world, is the price of happiness.

It is paradoxical that a work so authentically impregnated with charity should be at the same time the most anti-Christian of all Camus's books. For it obviously is a work which aims to prove most clearly that man can construct, without the help of God or of rationalistic thought, a creative humanism of high nobility. Wherever two or three people are gathered together, there is hope, Camus seems to say. However irremediable and definitive man's imprisonment, he can now rejoice in a sense of dignity and an innate feeling of sympathy that suffices to make him great.

CAMUS'S LIBERAL HUMANISM

The Rebel, Camus's second philosophical essay, furthers the line of thought adumbrated in *The Plague.* Revolt, in Camus's mind, is a creative effort that makes absurdity meaningful, or rather enables us to transcend absurdity, by protesting against it; it postulates a "human nature" that must be respected, a terrestrial brotherhood that must be defended; and it creates a moral value rooted in the idea of moderation and the respect for limits.

As a matter of fact, the idea of revolt is at the very heart of Camus's thinking. It is the key at once to his notion of happiness and the meaning of life as well as the purpose of social action and artistic creation.

In many ways, Camus is restating the basic principles of liberal humanism. In a deeper sense, he is exploring and justifying the immense potential man has for becoming himself. The Christian might profitably take up where Camus leaves off to examine the implications of this vision in respect to his own situation in this world. It would be too much to say that his position can be adopted without modification as a basis for Christian humanism. But it has merits that command our interest. Camus is not unique in his preoccupation with the absurd. What makes him unique, and what stirs sentiments of admiration in those who read him, is the courage and logic with which he refuses to compromise the dignity of man.

Crime and the Anarchist in *The Plague*

Robert R. Brock

Robert R. Brock is a professor of French and the humanities who teaches at the University of Montana. In this selection, Brock explores the theory of modern anarchy. In his discussion, Brock debunks misconceptions of violence and terrorism that are associated with the theory. Analyzing the political theme of anarchy in *The Plague*, Brock demonstrates how it is expressed by Camus through two of the important characters of the novel, Tarrou and Cottard. Through this perspective, Brock examines the issue of crime and how it is viewed in an anarchic society.

A misunderstanding of the term "anarchist,". . . for Americans, conjures up comic-strip images of sinister men in long black cloaks carrying bombs with lighted fuses. It is my contention, however, that many elements of Camus's work, and the treatment of the criminal in particular, make more sense if examined in the light of French anarchist thought.

Two or three observations are in order at this point. First of all, although economic equality is of primary concern to the politically active anarchist, it is of no serious importance to Camus, who deals mainly with questions of individual liberty and responsibility. Second, although some terrorists call themselves anarchists, their penchant for violence is incompatible with basic French concepts of anarchism. Joseph Prudhon, the nineteenth-century theoretician and father of modern anarchist thought in France, used the word "anarchy" in the sense of its Greek root: an absence of authority or government. Although the connotation of "disorder" has been attached to the word in modern times, it is not part of the original meaning of the word. Prudhon believed that representative government, or any form of centrally di-

Excerpted from Robert R. Brock, "Crime and the Anarchist in *The Plague*," in *Approaches to Teaching Camus's* The Plague, edited by Steven G. Kellman. Copyright © 1985 The Modern Language Association of America. Reprinted with permission from The Modern Language Association of America.

rected government, should be abolished and that the people should govern themselves in what amounts to pure participatory democracy. Thus, in the absence of central authority, it is the duty of each person to participate both as an individual and as a committee member in the management of public affairs. Such participation must ensure not only the common good but also the total personal liberty of each member of the society. For that is the key idea: total personal liberty. This concept is the closest thing the anarchists have to a dogma. It is so strongly held that anarchists who are unable to accept any given decisions of their committees have the right to withdraw from the committees, without prejudice, and not to return until they can do so with a clear conscience. In case of conflict between personal liberty and the general welfare, anarchists believe that the general welfare will eventually prevail since, again in their opinion, human beings are self-perfectable. It is the belief in total personal liberty that prevents the true anarchist from indulging in violence since to do so would deprive others of their right to liberty, including the right to hold dissenting opinions.

With these concepts of personal liberty and duty in mind, I open the discussion of *The Plague* by examining Rambert, the Parisian journalist. Rambert is determined to leave Oran, even at the risk of spreading the plague, in order to rejoin the woman he loves. He asks Dr. Rieux if he is wrong in preferring his own happiness to all other considerations, in particular the general welfare of others. He is also worried that Rieux will inform the police of his intentions. Since Rambert could spread the disease that Rieux is trying to control, the doctor's seemingly irresponsible attitude may well seem incomprehensible to us. From an anarchist's standpoint, however, Rieux must state that Rambert is *not* wrong (note that he does not say that Rambert is right), because Rambert has an absolute right to his personal liberty. Moreover, Rieux cannot inform the police since he might thereby contribute to the suppression of Rambert's liberty and an anarchist simply cannot assume that responsibility. Rambert's dilemma, the conflict between his personal desires and the common good, is rather neatly resolved by his deciding to stay in Oran and join a nonofficial committee that is fighting the plague. At the same time, two anarchist principles have been demonstrated: Rambert has made the proper choice of the general welfare, and he has become a participant in public activities. A third principle has been demonstrated by Rieux's attitude: faith in one's fellows.

THE PUNISHMENT OF CRIME IS A CRIME

Nonetheless, the concept of total individual liberty does pose a problem: the potential abuse of that liberty. Since there is no anarchist dogma, it is impossible to think "wrong," as we saw with Rambert. It is possible, however, to act wrongly by depriving others of their liberty. Anarchist thinking holds that no one will be truly free until all are free, the ultimate goal of anarchism. To punish me by imprisoning me for acting improperly is to deprive me of my liberty. Since depriving me of my liberty is wrong, the very punishment of crime is a crime. It is for this reason that Camus, discussing judges in *The Rebel*, states that these representatives of "justice" have chosen crime for themselves when they punish others and that unless they can prove their own innocence, which is impossible, the prisons must be emptied. Although the anarchists believe that human beings are self-perfectable, the problem to be faced until that millennium arrives is what to do about those who fail to respect the liberty of others. Not surprisingly, anarchist writers do not dwell at great length on that subject.

Bakunin, a nineteenth-century Russian anarchist and disciple of Prudhon, states that criminal acts are to be considered a manifestation of an illness and that punishment is to be a cure rather than society's traditional reprisal. Maurice Joyeux, a contemporary French theoretician and, O paradox, a sometime candidate for the French presidency, simply states that human beings are not guilty, that is, not guilty of anything. According to Joyeux, individuals are the way they are either by chance or God's design, depending on one's personal beliefs. In either case, since they have not transgressed by choice, they are innocent and do not merit traditional punishment. Since they retain their right to total personal liberty, they have the right to refuse punishment. Indeed, Prudhon believed that criminals should agree to punishment only if they felt that it would benefit them. Criminals can refuse punishment by declaring that they no longer wish to be a part of their particular society or group. The group then has the right to exile them. . . .

It is obvious early in *The Plague* that Cottard is a criminal. Clear indications include his distress at the prospect of having his botched suicide attempt reported to the police and his question to Dr. Rieux about whether the police have a right to arrest a person ill in a hospital. Even more interesting is his storming out of the tobacconist's shop after the woman's statement that "trash" like the commercial employee who had killed an Arab on the beach near Algiers should be thrown into prison. The commercial employee would seem to be Meursault from *The Stranger* (*L'Etranger*), who did shoot an Arab on a beach near Algiers. Since I believe that Camus has brought Meursault into the story, I feel that it is proper for me to review his case. I point out that Meursault, a European, was brought to trial for having shot an Arab who had pulled a knife on him in a land where, before World War II, Arabs had precious few rights. I add that, in my opinion, since the Arab had no family that we see and no friends at the trial and did not even have a name, he was not really a character but a pretext. That is, someone had to be sentenced to die to enable Camus to write a polemic against the death penalty. By ignoring the Arab and placing all the emphasis on Meursault, Camus has given us not a criminal but a victim, a victim of traditional justice. Cottard is treated in much the same manner. We do not know of what crime he stands accused; we know simply that it was not murder. Instead we see his anguish, his pathetic attempts to create a new personage for himself, and we note that while he is not particularly admirable, neither is he despicable. Moreover, once the gates of Oran are shut, Cottard is very effectively in exile with past crimes abolished and a chance to mend his ways.

BEARING THE PLAGUE AND APPROVING OF DEATH

Once the place and importance of Cottard are established, we examine Camus's use of the plague as a metaphor for World War II with its collective guilt (Paneloux's sermon), isolation, crematoriums, and so on. The next important discussion of crime and the anarchist viewpoint comes with Tarrou's confession. As in *The Stranger* we again have a prosecuting attorney, Tarrou's father, demanding the guillotine for an accused criminal, and again, there is not one word about the alleged crimes of this man Camus describes as a "frightened owl." In fact, Tarrou felt that the man was guilty but "of what crime is no matter." In reaction to that execution and the society that demanded it, Tarrou becomes a political activist, approving policies he knows will lead to the deaths of others. It is only later, while again witnessing an execution, that Tarrou is forced to recognize that he is no different from his father. Despite all the brave words about a perfect society where there will be no more killing, men have been sentenced to death and he has approved.

The plague is now a metaphor not only for passing the death sentence but also for approving the consequent deaths. It matters not whether the "dirty mouths stinking of plague" belong to the red robes or the revolutionaries. Tarrou sees them all as being plague bearers and refuses further association with those who, for good reasons or bad, bring death to others or justify their deaths. Since, in Tarrou's mind, all systems approve of at least some deaths for what are perceived to be good reasons and since Tarrou cannot approve of the taking of life under any circumstances, there can be only one logical solution: refuse all systems. That is, become an anarchist.

As the epidemic draws to a close, Cottard and Tarrou meet for the last time. Cottard is upset at the prospect of the quarantine's being lifted because it means his exile will be over and he will again be subject to arrest for his past crimes. He tells Tarrou that it would be great to be able to begin anew with a "clean sheet." But he had already been given that chance when the gates were first shut, and he had refused it. Not only did he deal in the black market, he had approved of the plague, saying that it suited him perfectly well, and had refused participation in the sanitary squads, the nonofficial committees formed by Tarrou. When two men, obviously plain-clothesmen, ask him if his name is Cottard, he takes flight, later barricading himself in his room and firing on people in the street. If we read these pages carefully, we again note the anarchist mind at work. First of all, it is not possible for Cottard to be truly guilty of a crime. According to Tarrou, his only real crime is having approved of that which kills children and adults, and in one policeman's opinion, later echoed by Grand, he's gone mad. Second, when they take him alive, one of the officers strikes him in the face twice and then kicks him when he falls to the ground. This gratuitous brutality, more than a little reminiscent of the scene in *The Stranger* where the officer slaps Raymond Sintès, ensures that the reader will sympathize with Cottard and not with the police. Had they killed him in a shoot-out, they would have been acting in self-defense, and the reader's sympathies would have been with that most immediate and disliked symbol of authority, the police.

In all this, we see Cottard do but a single mean thing; he shoots a stray dog. The incident has no real importance in the story, and certainly no connection with anarchism, but it intrigues by its very gratuitousness. It is as though Camus were amusing himself by giving us a little puzzle to solve. Taking it in that vein, we note that the dog Cottard shoots is a spaniel and that there is at least one other spaniel in Camus's work: the one Salamano loses in *The Stranger* in another Algerian city, Algiers. I find a fair amount of rather grim humor in the description of the dog's wandering down the street and stopping to scratch its fleas, and even in the description of its grotesque death throes. As to why Camus would indulge in such a diversion, the answer is probably in the long discussion between Tarrou and Rieux: one cannot fight the plague all the time, one has to have a simple pleasure or two. Tarrou and Rieux go for a swim.

Tarrou has long since recognized that he is a plague bearer and has attempted to redeem himself. He will not be a part of a legal governing body, but he will organize an unofficial committee, the sanitary squads, to serve the common good. Where the government would use conscripts, Tarrou will accept only volunteers since participation will probably amount to a death sentence and one has the right to choose that only for one's self. The choice to serve is to be seen not as heroic but simply as necessary for the common good. Tarrou's actions concretize yet again the anarchist belief in the perfectability of humankind. That is, properly instructed and enlightened, men and women will become altruistic, preferring, like Rambert, the general welfare to their own personal well being.

As Dr. Rieux continues his rounds, he thinks not of his dead friend Tarrou but of Cottard and the fists smashing Cottard's face, because as Camus notes, it is "harder to think of a guilty man than a dead one." But, in keeping with anarchist principles, there are no guilty characters in the book. At worst, Cottard is culpable of selfishness, hardly a real crime. And in this allegory of World War II, not only are the rats innocent of any wrongdoing, there is no evil genius to have unleashed them. Like Prudhon and Bakunin before him, Camus prefers to dwell on the positive aspects of human nature in its striving for a better world.

Chronology

1913

Albert Camus is born to Lucien Auguste Camus and Catherine Sintès in Mondovi, Algeria, on November 7; he is the couple's second son.

1914

Catherine, Albert, and brother Lucien move to the home of Catherine's mother, Marie Catherine Sintès, in the Belcourt district of Algiers when Albert's father is reactivated into military service after the outbreak of World War I. In October, Albert's father dies from wounds suffered in the Battle of the Marne.

1914–1918

Camus's family lives in poor conditions, sharing a home with his maternal grandmother and two uncles. Catherine works as a charwoman, and her mother helps to raise her sons.

1918–1923

Camus begins his elementary education, guided by a concerned teacher, Louis Germain, who personally coaches his student to qualify for a scholarship to attend high school; the scholarship allays the financial worries of Camus's family, and his grandmother allows him to continue his education.

1924–1932

Camus attends high school in Algiers, where he excels at soccer and develops an abiding interest in composition, literature, and philosophy. Jean Grenier, a philosophy teacher from France, becomes Camus's mentor; the two would remain lifelong friends.

1930

Camus becomes seriously ill and is diagnosed with tuberculosis.

1931

During his recuperation, Camus postpones his studies and moves into the home of his uncle and aunt, Gustave and Antoinette Acault. Gustave cultivates his nephew's intellectual development by introducing him to important works of literature and philosophy. Marie Sintès dies.

1932–1933

Camus studies with Grenier in the preparatory program for the university. He publishes his first articles in the local journal, *Sud.*

1934–1936

Camus attends the University of Algiers and develops an interest in left-wing politics.

1934

Camus marries Simone Hié on June 16; her addiction to morphine is an obstacle in the couple's relationship.

1935

Camus joins the French Communist Party and begins serving as the secretary-general of the Algiers Cultural Center. He begins work on a collection of essay-novellas titled *The Wrong Side and the Right Side.*

1936

After writing his thesis, Camus graduates from the university with a degree in philosophy; his tubercular condition rules out teacher certification. Camus helps found a politically active performance troupe, the Théâtre du Travail, and becomes involved in all aspects of its productions. An emotionally disastrous trip to Europe precipitates the separation of Simone and Camus, and he begins to draft a novel, *A Happy Death.*

1937

Camus publishes *The Wrong Side and the Right Side.* He is expelled from the Communist Party after disagreements over the Algerian independence movement. Camus founds the Théâtre de L'Equipe, meets Francine Faure, travels to Europe, and begins drafting *The Stranger.*

1938–1939

Camus starts his career in journalism by working as an editor and writer for the new left-wing newspapers *Alger Républicain* and *Le Soir Républicain,* for which he writes articles on political and social issues as well as book reviews. He begins composing *The Myth of Sisyphus* and *Caligula,* and he publishes *Nuptials* (1939), a collection of lyrical prose. World War II begins, and Camus tries to enlist for military service but is refused because of his health.

1940

The *Alger Républicain* and *Le Soir Républicain* fold under pressure from the Algerian governor-general. Camus moves to France to work as an editor for *Paris-Soir*. The German forces occupy France, and Camus is relocated to Lyons, where he is joined by Faure; they marry on December 3. Camus is fired from *Paris-Soir*.

1941

Camus and Francine move to Oran, Algeria. Camus alternates between Oran and Algiers, works as a tutor, and begins composing *The Plague*. His manuscripts for *The Stranger*, *The Myth of Sisyphus*, and *Caligula* are circulated by his friend and former editor Pascal Pia to important writers and editors at the Éditions Gallimard publishing house.

1942

Éditions Gallimard publishes *The Stranger*. Camus suffers a relapse of tuberculosis and moves to Le Panelier, located in a mountainous region of France, to recover. Camus and Francine are separated on opposite sides of enemy lines when the Allies liberate Algeria and the Germans conquer unoccupied France.

1943

The Myth of Sisyphus is published. Camus associates with members of the French resistance movement in Le Panelier. By the end of the year, Camus is living in Paris, working as a reader at Éditions Gallimard while secretly participating in the resistance as a writer and editor for the underground newspaper *Combat*. He meets Jean-Paul Sartre and begins associating with his intellectual circle.

1944

Camus continues his resistance activities. His play *The Misunderstanding* is produced and receives mixed reviews. The play features the actress Maria Casarès, with whom Camus begins an affair. Paris is liberated in August, and Camus is awarded the Resistance Medal for his work on *Combat*, which begins to publish openly. Francine joins Camus in Paris.

1945

Casarès ends her affair with Camus. Francine gives birth to twins Jean and Catherine on September 5. Camus's play

Caligula is produced and receives better reviews than his last production.

1946

Camus travels to the United States on a cultural relations tour, lecturing and promoting the new American edition of *The Stranger.* He continues to associate with important literary figures, including Sartre, Simone de Beauvoir, André Malraux, André Gide, and Arthur Koestler.

1947

The Plague is published in June and becomes a best-seller. Following its release, Camus withdraws from *Combat* after a bitter falling out with Pascal Pia. Camus begins to disagree with many of his leftist intellectual friends who sympathize with the Communists; he starts to compose *The Rebel.*

1948

Camus returns to the theater with a new play, *State of Siege,* which is met by the critics with nearly universal contempt; he resumes his affair with Casarès.

1949

Camus travels to South America on a cultural relations tour for the French foreign ministry; he returns after suffering more serious bouts of tuberculosis. His play *The Just Assassins* is produced in December, featuring Casarès.

1950

Camus continues working at Éditions Gallimard, where he directs his own line of titles, which includes works by Carl Jung and Federico García Lorca. He compiles a number of his own political journalistic articles, many on the subject of Algeria, in *Actuelles I.*

1951–1952

The Rebel is published (late in 1951), and is the center of controversy among the left-wing intellectual community. In a series of articles, Sartre and his staff harshly criticize the work. Camus responds, and Sartre formally announces the end of their friendship.

1953

Actuelles II is published. Camus travels to Italy, Greece, and Algeria. Francine suffers from depression.

1954–1955

Camus publishes *Summer,* a collection of lyrical essays. During a visit to Oran, he restrains Francine from a possible suicide attempt. Francine is kept under observation in French clinics, where she receives electroshock therapy that does not improve her condition. Terrorist violence erupts in Algeria when an independence movement targets French colonialists. Camus is invited to voice his opinions on Algerian independence in *L'Express*.

1956

Camus goes to Algeria to negotiate a civilian truce, but no one is interested in his proposed solutions. His moderate position on Algerian independence is scorned by his peers, and he becomes ostracized from the French intellectual and literary circles. Camus resigns from *L'Express* and publishes a novel, *The Fall*, which is well received despite the resentment of his enemies. He begins a letter-writing campaign to win freedom for political prisoners in Algeria. Camus adapts and produces William Faulkner's novel *Requiem for a Nun* for the stage.

1957

Camus receives the Nobel Prize for literature; he and Francine travel to Stockholm, Sweden, for the awards ceremony. *Exile and the Kingdom*, a collection of novellas, is published.

1958

Actuelles III is published. Camus continues his private letter-writing campaign to win pardons for men condemned to the death penalty. He suffers from tubercular respiratory difficulties.

1959

Camus adapts and produces Fyodor Dostoyevsky's novel *The Possessed* for the stage. He alternates between Paris and his new home in rural Lourmarin, where he begins composing the novel *The First Man*.

1960

Returning to Paris from Lourmarin with his publisher, Michel Gallimard, Camus is killed in a car accident on January 4. A manuscript for *The First Man* is found at the scene of the accident.

1971

Camus's early unfinished novel, *A Happy Death*, is published posthumously.

1979

Francine Faure Camus dies.

1994

Camus's daughter, Catherine, publishes *The First Man*.

For Further Research

Works by Camus Readily Available in English Translation

Between Hell and Reason: Essays from the Resistance Newspaper "Combat," 1944–1947. Trans. Alexandre de Gramont. Middletown, CT: Wesleyan University Press, 1991.

"Caligula" and Three Other Plays. Trans. Stuart Gilbert. New York: Random House, 1962.

Exile and the Kingdom. Ed. Erroll McDonald. New York: Vintage Books, 1991.

The Fall. Trans. Justin O'Brien. New York: Vintage Books, 1991.

The First Man. Trans. David Hapgood. New York: Vintage Books, 1996.

A Happy Death. Trans. Richard Howard. New York: Vintage Books, 1995.

Lyrical and Critical Essays. Trans. Ellen Conroy Kennedy. New York: Random House, 1995.

"The Myth of Sisyphus" and Other Essays. Trans. Justin O'Brien. New York: Vintage Books, 1991.

Notebooks, 1935–1951. Trans. Philip Malcolm Waller Thody and Justin O'Brien. New York: Marlowe, 1998.

The Plague. Trans. Stuart Gilbert. New York: Vintage Books, 1991.

The Rebel: An Essay on Man in Revolt. Ed. Erroll McDonald. New York: Vintage Books, 1991.

Resistance, Rebellion, and Death. Trans. Justin O'Brien. New York, 1995.

The Stranger. Trans. Matthew Ward. New York: Vintage Books, 1989.

170   *Readings on* The Plague

Youthful Writings. Trans. Ellen Conroy Kennedy. New York: Knopf, 1976.

ABOUT CAMUS'S WORKS

Alba Amoia, *Albert Camus.* New York: Continuum, 1989.

Harold Bloom, ed., *Albert Camus.* New York: Chelsea House, 1989.

Germaine Brée, ed., *Camus: A Collection of Critical Essays.* Englewood Cliffs, NJ: Prentice- Hall, 1962.

John Cruickshank, *Albert Camus and the Literature of Revolt.* Wesport, CT: Greenwood, 1978.

David R. Ellison, *Understanding Albert Camus.* Columbia: University of South Carolina Press, 1990.

Steven G. Kellman, ed., *Approaches to Teaching Camus's "The Plague."* New York: Modern Language Association of America, 1985.

Bettina L. Knapp, ed., *Critical Essays on Albert Camus.* Boston: G.K. Hall, 1988.

Brian Masters, *Camus: A Study.* London: Heinemann, 1974.

Conor Cruise O'Brien, *Albert Camus of Europe and Asia.* New York: Viking, 1970.

Philip H. Rhein, *Albert Camus.* Boston: Twayne, 1989.

David Sprintzen, *Camus: A Critical Study.* Philadelphia: Temple University Press, 1988.

BIOGRAPHIES OF CAMUS

Germaine Brée, *Camus.* New Brunswick, NJ: Rutgers University Press, 1961.

Herbert P. Lottman, *Albert Camus: A Biography.* Garden City, NY: Doubleday, 1979.

Patrick McCarthy, *Camus.* New York: Random House, 1982.

Philip Thody, *Albert Camus: 1913–1960.* New York: Macmillan, 1961.

Oliver Todd, *Albert Camus: A Life.* Trans. Benjamin Ivry. New York: Knopf, 1997.

INDEX